AN INTRODUCTION TO

BIRDS

by
JOHN KIERAN

Illustrations by Don Eckelberry

GARDEN CITY PUBLISHING CO., INC.

Garden City, New York

INDEX

INTRODUCTION

This is a book for beginners and has been made as simple as possible. It is offered as a help in learning to know the more common birds of our lawns, our fields, our woods, our waterways and our ocean shores. The way the birds are described in this book is not the way in which a scientist would describe them, nor is the order in which the bird pictures are shown the order in which a scientist would place them. There is a reason for that. Sometimes in a theater program the names of those in the cast are listed in order of their appearance on the stage. That's about the way it is with the birds in this book. They are listed more or less in the general order in which you might expect to see them if you stepped outside the door and began to look around for common birds.

Later on, when the beginner has learned something about birds in this simple fashion, he or she will be better able to understand why the scientists list birds as they do, placing them in what they call Orders, Families, Genera and Species. There are many fine books on such subjects, with detailed descriptions, life histories and colored plates of all the birds of North America. They have been written by famous field experts and illustrated by noted bird painters. But the very wealth of the material in many of these handbooks and heavier volumes may baffle or—worse still—discourage the beginner. The modest aim here is to provide the novice with an elementary guide to a friendly acquaintance with the more common of our native birds of North America. After that the reader may move ahead to wider and richer fields.

The first rule to follow if you want to know the birds is: Look at them! I put it that way because I remember the time I discovered that I had been going about the woods and fields without seeing the many birds that were all around me. It was when I was teaching school in Dutchess County, New York. I had a one-room schoolhouse in the woods and six pupils who were farm children. Among other things, I was supposed to teach them how to recognize a few common birds. I had been supplied with colored pictures of four birds that were to be made known to the children that year and under each picture was a short account of the bird—its name, its habits and when and where to look for it.

The first one of these bird cards that I looked at pictured an odd bird in a queer position. The bird was gray and black on top and clear white underneath, and it seemed to be going down a fence post headfirst. That surprised me. I never had seen any bird going down a fence post or a tree trunk headfirst. I thought that perhaps I had the picture upside down, so I turned it the other way around. But then the writing on the card was upside down. It was evident that the bird was meant to be shown going down the fence post headfirst. I read what was on the card. It said that the bird was the White-breasted Nuthatch, a common bird that was noted for its habit of going down tree trunks, telegraph poles or fence posts headfirst and that most farm children were familiar with it.

I was puzzled. The bird was absolutely new to me, though I had been walking along the roads, over the fields and through the woods of that region since I had been a small boy myself. I thought I knew something about birds in a general way. I certainly knew a Robin and a Bluebird and a Crow and a Baltimore Oriole and a few more. But here was a "common bird"—the card had it in plain print—that I never had seen in my life! I made up my mind to look for it, since the card stated that it was a "permanent resident," a bird that stayed around all year. I said nothing to my pupils about birds that afternoon. I went home to sleep on the matter.

I slept out on the open porch of our farmhouse. The first thing I saw when I woke up the next morning—a frosty October morning—was this bird, the White-breasted Nuthatch, going headfirst down the trunk of a black cherry tree about ten feet from the end of my nose. I had to walk about a mile to reach the school and on the way to school that morning I kept my eyes open and saw four more of these odd-looking birds moving up, down and around the trunks and large branches of trees. By the time I reached the school door I realized that the birds always had been there but I never had looked at them. I hadn't seen what was before my eyes. In short, I had been blind! I made up my mind to look for birds after that. I am still looking and having a lot of fun finding them. I have learned to recognize many of our native North American birds and so can anyone else who keeps his eyes open, looks around him and takes accurate note of what he sees.

That's an important point—to note accurately what you see. Many times I have been asked to give the names of birds that other persons have seen and have tried to describe to me. But most of the time they described birds that never existed on land or sea. Those persons were not good observers. They saw things that were not there. They missed things they should have seen. I'm not sure what is the first question to ask a person who has seen a bird and wants to know its name from his description, but there are a few important questions that, if answered correctly, very quickly narrow down the search for the name of any native bird that has been seen in the open.

One such question is: Where did you see this bird? There are birds of the ocean shores, birds of the fields, birds of the woods. If we know where a bird was seen, we are closer to solving the problem of what bird it might have been that was seen there. The next question might be: How big was this bird? In a marsh, for instance, the difference in size may vary from that of the Marsh Wrens only 4 or 5 inches in length to that of the Great Blue Heron standing more than 3 feet tall. Incidentally, the actual size of the birds listed in this book is indicated by the length in inches printed under the name of each bird. The measurement is from the tip of the bill to the tip of the tail when head, tail and body are placed in a straight line, as they are in the "bird skins" that are preserved for study in museums. A field method for beginners easier than trying to estimate the actual length of a strange bird is to note whether it is a little larger or smaller than some well-known bird such as an English Sparrow or a Robin. The size in inches can come later.

When we know where the bird was seen and have an estimate of its size, we can ask about the color and the markings and begin to close in upon the mysterious stranger. It still must be remembered that, in the case of many birds, the female doesn't look like the male, the young may differ from both parents, and there are decided changes in plumage in many species according to the season of the year. The beginner is not expected to grasp all these differences in a hurry. Even the expert is sometimes baffled by the Autumn traveling plumage of some of the smaller migrants—like the Wood Warblers—unless he has a prolonged view in good light of the bird in question.

But once we know where the bird was seen, its size and its color and markings, a few more questions and answers may solve the problem. If the bird was seen in the air, how did it fly? Did it have a rapid or a slow wing motion? Did it flap its wings steadily or did it flutter, sail a bit and then flutter the wings again? Was its flight level or did it seem to go bounding through the air? If the bird was on the ground, did it hop, walk or run when it moved about? Did it have a long tail or a short tail? Did it wag its tail nervously or bob its head when it walked? What was the shape of its bill—long, short, thick, thin?

It's probable that the beginner, at first, will miss many of these points, but they are picked up quickly. It is no time at all before the novice notices that Sparrows hop, Robins run and Blackbirds walk when they are feeding on the ground. There are birds that often chatter or sing while on the wing and other birds that are always silent while flying. In some cases birds are more easily recognized by sound than by sight. Often you can hear a bird that you can't see. As a matter of fact, it is much easier to hear some birds than to see them. The Whip-poor-will, for instance. There are many persons who have heard the vibrant throbbing call of "Whip-poor-WILL, Whip-poor-WILL!" in the gathering dusk of a country evening and still can say of the unseen singer in the oncoming night as Wordsworth said of the Cuckoo of his native England:

Even yet thou are to me
No bird, but an invisible thing,
A voice, a mystery.

Owls are more often heard than seen. It is a rare thing for me to see a Barred Owl, but we have exchanged hoots in a clearing in the woods on many a moonless night. The Black-crowned Night Heron was just a hoarse squawk in the darkness to me for years. I never had seen a Grasshopper Sparrow until one day, on the farm, I read in Chapman's *Handbook of Birds of Eastern North America* how many persons overlooked this bird because its song was so much like the buzzing of a grasshopper that they never bothered to look in that direction for a bird. Immediately I recalled hearing a sound like that in a nearby hayfield that very morning. I went out with my binoculars, heard the sound, looked in that direction and found my first Grasshopper Sparrow buzzing away merrily from the top of a Curly Dock plant.

Which brings up the matter of field glasses. For recognizing some of the smaller birds—Sparrows and Warblers, for instance—there is no doubt that field glasses eventually are needed. But a good start can be made without binoculars simply by going out and keeping eyes and ears always on the alert. Getting to know a bird by sight is the only sure way of making new acquaintances, but linking the song to the singer is the easiest way of finding old friends that have come back to your neighborhood. Walk softly and slowly. Be patient. When you think there is no longer any hope that the bird is in the vicinity, take one more look. Stand perfectly still for minutes on end if you think there is a chance that there are shy birds near you. Birds are frightened by sudden movements more than they are by loud noises.

Above all, do not be discouraged if you make mistakes at first. All beginners make ludicrous errors. It takes time to learn anything, particularly the birds, which are known to be flighty creatures. The pictures in this book are, for the most part, of the males in breeding plumage, which is their brightest dress. Meeting the birds this way is merely the first step in coming to know the birds well, but it is, I think, the easiest step and at the same time the most important step. Once you have taken this step, you may go as far as you please.

But why bother at all to know the birds? What will it profit any person to have an interest in birds? Well, for one thing, birds play a considerable part in vermin and insect control on our farms and thus help our fruit and grain crops to come to fuller harvest. The more important point to most of us is that acquaintance with birds provides a fuller and richer life for any individual. Art and Literature, from the beginning of human history, have been studded with bird lore. The names of many birds can be traced back to beautiful Greek legends. In the Bible we find mention of the Dove that brought good news to Noah's Ark, the Ravens that fed Elijah, and many other birds. There were the cackling Geese that saved ancient Rome from surprise in a night attack and the Gulls that saved the lives of the Mormon founders of modern Salt Lake City, wherefor there is a beautiful monument to the Gulls in that city. Shakespeare never wrote a play without scattering bird notes through it. Keats dedicated immortal lines to the Nightingale and Shelley wrote wildly well of the Skylark. Raphael painted the Madonna of the Goldfinch. St. Francis of Assisi preached to the birds. We have ancient, honorable, artistic and religious authority for taking an interest in the birds around us. It's a pursuit that is good for body and soul. Who loves and knows the birds will never lack for company outdoors and, wherever he may go by land or sea, will be finding old friends and meeting new friends all the days of his life.

ROBIN
(About 10 inches)

Everybody knows the Robin Redbreast, a familiar bird all over North America. In Canada and most of the United States except the Gulf Coast area they are "Summer residents." That is, they come with the warm weather of Spring and leave when "the North Wind doth blow and we shall have snow." Some hardy Robins may stay through the season of snow and ice, but if we look out the window in late February or early March and see a Robin on our lawn, most of us are inclined to shout: "Spring has come; the Robins are back!" They are friendly, trusting birds and feel quite at home on our lawns. Notice that they do not walk when they move about the ground; they run. Male and female are alike in general color but the female is usually a little duller than the handsome male Robin and young Robins have spotted breasts like their near relatives, the Thrushes. Robins have a rolling carol that is cheerful and melodious. They like to take baths and a bird bath on your lawn will bring Robins to bathe in it. Note that the length of the Robin—from the tip of its bill to the tip of its tail—is about 10 inches. Since the Robin is so well known, it can be used as a guide to help identify other birds by the difference in size or plumage between the stranger and the Robin.

ENGLISH SPARROW
(About 6 inches)

This bird is called the English Sparrow because it was brought here from England about 100 years ago, but it is common all over Europe, just as it has become common all over this country. It is a familiar sight in cities and suburbs and around our farmyards where it chirps, chatters, fights and builds its nests in all sorts of places, high and low, in boxes, under eaves, in cornices, in old shoes, drain spouts, gutters and other odd lodgings. Its plumage is often discolored by dust and smoke in cities, but around a farmyard it is surprising how nice the male looks in its clean suit. The male is the one with the large black bib tucked under its chin. The female and young are duller in color. English Sparrows are hardy, chunky, noisy, rowdy and cheerful. They have driven off many of our Bluebirds and Purple Martins by taking their nesting sites but otherwise are settling down as regular residents and accepted members of the bird community.

STARLING
(About 8 inches)

The plumage of the Starling varies according to the time of year, but the shape and actions of this bird are enough to distinguish it from such other blackish birds as Grackles, Cowbirds and Rusty Blackbirds that also walk about our pastures and lawns. At all times the Starling is the chunky, heavy-shouldered bird with the short tail and the longish bill. In the Spring the bill of the male is yellow, which easily sets it apart from our other black birds. The plumage of the birds at that season is a shining mixture of brown, black, green and dark blue that glistens in the sunlight. In the Autumn and Winter the Starlings have speckled or mottled plumage. They are not natives of this country. They were brought over from Europe, and the descendants of Starlings that were imported in 1892 and liberated in Central Park in New York City have spread from the Atlantic Coast to the Rocky Mountains. In time they will cover the whole country, because nothing seems to stop them. They feed in flocks, walking about in zigzag fashion as if they didn't care which way they were going. They breed in holes or cornices of buildings, raise two or three broods a year and are looked upon as nuisances where they become too numerous. They have a wonderful variety of whistles, squeaks and call notes and can imitate the songs of dozens of native birds.

BLUE JAY
(About 12 inches)

The handsome, swaggering, noisy Blue Jay wears a striking costume of sky-blue over-sprinkled with stripes and patches of midnight black and clear white. It has a sharp crest, a sharp voice and a sharp eye for everything that goes on in the neighborhood. It patrols the highways and byways, bullying smaller birds, heckling stray cats, shrieking at any hawks or owls it may spy and generally looking into the business of any stranger in the vicinity. The ordinary note of the Blue Jay is a jeering cry but it can produce many other sounds, including some flute-like notes, a nut-cracking noise and a perfect imitation of the whistling cry of the Red-shouldered Hawk. There are half a dozen kinds of Jays in different parts of the country, but the Blue Jay is the most common and the most widespread. It ranges from the Atlantic Coast to the Rocky Mountains and there are few birds with which it might be confused. The Belted Kingfisher is probably the closest in appearance to the Blue Jay. Both birds are largely blue and white and both have crests. Also, they are about the same size. But the Belted Kingfisher is a short-tailed, short-legged, heavy-bodied bird with a jagged crest and a very heavy bill, whereas the Blue Jay is a graceful, sharp-crested, long-tailed bird that is much more common around our fields and woods. The Belted Kingfisher sticks pretty close to ponds, lakes and rivers.

CROW
(About 19 inches)

The "black Crow" is all black—wings, body, head, feet and beak—and some persons go on to say that it has a disposition to match its color. Farmers put up "scarecrows" to keep these birds out of their cornfields and there are organized "Crow shoots" in some localities to reduce their numbers, but Crows flourish just the same. Probably that's because they are wary birds. When Crows are feeding in a field they usually have at least one sentinel posted on a lofty perch to give warning of any approaching danger. They can say "Caw" in a dozen different ways, and each variation has a different meaning to them. They can make other sounds, too, including a cracking, stuttering sound like the creaking of a heavy barn door on rusty hinges. They have the bad habit of robbing cornfields and they are also charged with the crime of raiding the nests and eating the eggs and young of smaller birds. It is probable that this crime is more often attempted than carried out because Crows often are seen being driven away from nests of infuriated small birds. Crows definitely do much good by eating many slugs, beetles and caterpillars that do damage in gardens, grainfields and orchards. Whether they are a helpful or a harmful bird is a great subject of debate. Perhaps they are helpful in some regions and harmful in others.

What is certain about Crows is that they are very interesting birds. They are the watchmen of the woods and the open fields. They gather in wheeling and cawing flocks whenever one of them spies a Hawk, an Owl, a fox or a jackrabbit. They will follow a fox across open country like a pack of winged hounds and drive an Owl from one evergreen tree to another by continued swooping at it. In return for this noisy attention, a fox will gladly eat a Crow if it can catch the bird off guard on the ground, and more than one Crow has been caught napping by a Great Horned Owl. Young Crows make good pets and are easily tamed but they are great thieves and will fly off with anything they can carry. It is not true that they can be taught to speak if you split their tongues. The Crow never uses its tongue in producing any sound that it can make.

Crows are birds of the fields and woods and it is hard to get near them. They usually nest in a high tree in the woods and it is believed that both parents share in the labor of hatching the eggs and bringing up the young birds, but it's hard to be sure because the male and female look exactly alike and it's difficult to know which one is on the nest or bringing in food at any particular time. Apart from the breeding season Crows often gather in great flocks and move to favorite roosting places in long lines at dusk. If disturbed on such roosts at night, the departing birds with their flapping wings sound like a great rush of water. All Crows look alike, but individually they are really odd characters.

BALTIMORE ORIOLE
(About 8 inches)

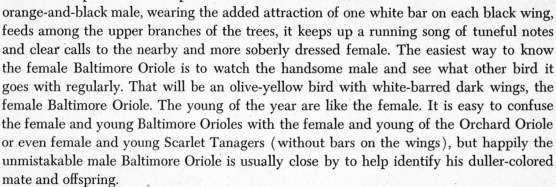

The beautiful, friendly and melodious Baltimore Oriole is easy to know because of its striking color combination of orange and black and its habit of feeding in the trees of our lawns, roadsides and orchards. It is a Summer resident of the eastern half of the United States and it is frequently in sight in the open all over its Summer range. It is not a bird of the deep woods. It likes the company of men, women and children and domestic animals like horses and cows. It loves to hang its wonderful woven nests in the outer foliage of our dooryard elms and our pasture-land maples and hickories. As the brilliant orange-and-black male, wearing the added attraction of one white bar on each black wing, feeds among the upper branches of the trees, it keeps up a running song of tuneful notes and clear calls to the nearby and more soberly dressed female. The easiest way to know the female Baltimore Oriole is to watch the handsome male and see what other bird it goes with regularly. That will be an olive-yellow bird with white-barred dark wings, the female Baltimore Oriole. The young of the year are like the female. It is easy to confuse the female and young Baltimore Orioles with the female and young of the Orchard Oriole or even female and young Scarlet Tanagers (without bars on the wings), but happily the unmistakable male Baltimore Oriole is usually close by to help identify his duller-colored mate and offspring.

It's the female that builds the remarkable hanging nests of this species and she does it by weaving plant fibers together so skillfully and efficiently that, long after the young birds have grown up and left home, the abandoned nests cling stubbornly to the bare branchlets through the rain, the snow, the sleet and the wild winds of Winter. Sometimes the birds conceal their nests so cleverly that we never find the woven cradle until the leaves come tumbling down in Autumn and bare the secret to the world at large. Many birds will accept contributions with thanks when they are looking for nesting material. Robins will take string or yarn of almost any color, but the female Baltimore Oriole prefers plain white yarn to weave into her nest along with grass and plant fibers. The 4 to 6 eggs hatch in about two weeks and there is only one brood a year as a rule.

Many years ago the poet Edgar Fawcett put in rhyme his admiration for the flashing Baltimore Oriole and asked:

> *At some glad moment was it Nature's choice*
> *To dower a scrap of sunset with a voice?*

But his final and delightful explanation of the origin of such a brilliant bird in our clime is that an orange-and-black tulip in an ancient garden

> *Yearning toward Heaven until its wish was heard,*
> *Desired unspeakably to be a bird.*

[14]

BROWN THRASHER
(About 11 inches)

The Brown Thrasher is a first cousin of the Mockingbird and Catbird and has the same general shape and good singing voice. It is the largest of the three and quite different in color from the others. The Brown Thrasher is a rich light brown with a reddish tinge above, and its cream-colored under parts are heavily marked by what look like dark dotted lines. It appears to be a "longish" bird because it has a long tail and a rather long bill that curves slightly downward. It can be found all over the United States in Summer, but in Winter the majority of the northern birds move southward to get away from the ice and snow. The Brown Thrasher is a bird of our lawns, shrubbery, village outskirts and farmlands. It is a fine singer with a loud clear voice and it picks a prominent perch—often the topmost branchlet of a tree or shrub—from which to perform. Some who have listened think they hear it say in Spring: "Plow now—plow now—plant it—drop it—cover it up—cover it up—good boy—three cheers!" It differs from the Thrushes in that it is a longer bird, has straw-colored eyes, has light wing bars and is much more a bird of the open fields and hedgerows.

CATBIRD
(About 9 inches)

The Catbird—general color a dark slate gray with a black cap and tail for those who look closer—is the poor relation of the Mockingbird. There are some who think that all a Catbird can do is mew like a cat and they refuse to believe that a bubbling song from the shrubbery can be produced by any Catbird. But the truth is that, while not quite up to the famous Mockingbird, it is a talented and tireless songster. It is not bold like a Blue Jay or easily familiar like a Robin. But it likes to live in the vicinity of houses and keep an eye on what people are doing. The Catbird is a skulking busybody, prying into everything, always lurking in the underbrush or peering out of the shrubbery. It builds a rather ramshackle nest in a thick bush and two broods a season are the rule. In the Summer there are Catbirds all over the United States east of the Rockies, but when the Autumn leaves come whirling down, most of the birds in the North pack up and go South to avoid the snows and wild winds of Winter. Catbirds feed mostly on insects but they will take a few berries in season. Still, we can't begrudge a few berries to such a beneficial and melodious bird.

[15]

RED-HEADED WOODPECKER
(About 9 inches)

Many Woodpeckers have some red on their heads, but this is the only one with an all-red head from the shoulders up. It is rare in eastern New York and New England and along the Pacific Coast, but elsewhere it is common and almost unmistakable because of the color combination, the bright red head and the contrasting black-and-white pattern—in large chunks—of the wings and body. The young have mottled brown heads but the large white patches in the black wings easily identify them. The older birds certainly are handsome and by no means shy. Male and female look alike and they catch the eye—or ear—as they fly from one dead branch to another or cling to a telegraph pole and utter their loud rattling calls. The golf courses of the country have turned out to be the favorite haunts of these brilliant birds. In fact, golf courses have become "bird sanctuaries" in general but the Red-headed Woodpecker, because of its size, color, loud cries and habit of alighting on dead limbs or fence posts, is one of the most easily noticed. Like other Woodpeckers, they breed in holes in trees or posts

HOUSE WREN
(About 5 inches)

There are more than a dozen different kinds of Wrens in North America, but you will have no trouble getting to know the House Wren. All Wrens have a family resemblance. They are small, stocky, brownish birds with lighter under parts, perky tails and small sharp bills, some of which curve slightly downward. To find most of them you have to go to special places such as the woods, the marshes, the canyons or the cactus lands. But the House Wren is well named. It likes to live in dooryards and, over the eastern half of the United States at least, rarely strays as far away as the orchard to build its nest. It will build in a convenient hole of any kind around the house or barn. It will build in the pocket of an old coat or in a mailbox or in a clothespin bag left hanging on the wash line. It carries twigs and grass to its nesting place and two or three broods a year are raised. The House Wren sings its rattling, rolling, bubbling song from daylight until dark. It is a bustling little bird, a spitfire. It is always feeding, fussing around, singing or driving away bigger birds that come near its nest. Our House Wrens move southward to spend the Winter near the Gulf of Mexico, but April or May always finds them back in our dooryards again.

CARDINAL
(About 8½ inches)

You couldn't mistake a male Cardinal for any other bird in North America. It is a flaming red bird—indeed, it is often called the Redbird—with a distinct crest and, around the base of its short and heavy red bill, it has a patch of black that extends back through the eye and down the throat a little way. The female Cardinal and the young of the year are much duller in color but they have the crest, the red bill and more than a hint of red in their cinnamon-yellow plumage to make them known as the wife and offspring of the more brilliant Cardinal. There is in the Southwest a bird, the Pyrrhuloxia, that is much like the female Cardinal (and young of the year) in size, color, shape and crest, but it has more gray in its plumage and it has a yellow bill, whereas all Cardinals have red bills.

In addition to that, the Pyrrhuloxia is confined to the mesquite and cactus regions of the Southwest, whereas the Cardinal is a cherished resident of most of the United States from the Canadian Border to the Gulf of Mexico and from the Atlantic Coast to the Rocky Mountains. It is uncommon in New England and rather rare on the Pacific Coast, but over the remainder of the country you may find it around villages or farms or any kind of open country, often whistling loudly and clearly from a perch on a telephone wire, a fence rail or the topmost branch of a tree. It sounds much like a boy whistling sharply for his dog. The female joins in the whistling, which is unusual among birds. Another mark of distinction for the Cardinal is—what most boys know—that it has a major league baseball club named after it; the St. Louis Cardinals.

Since the Cardinal usually is an all-year resident over its range, it has to live through the snows of Winter in the northerly part of the United States, and there is no prettier sight in Nature than a male Cardinal in a snow-covered setting, the fiery color of its plumage contrasting so vividly with the soft white background. Cardinals are beneficial as well as friendly and beautiful birds. They eat many weed seeds and no small amount of injurious insects of one kind or another, including the seventeen-year cicada or "locust." The female and young often lurk modestly in the shrubbery while the proud male is whistling loudly from an exposed perch, but the hidden members of the family give their presence away by the sharp "tsik" call note they utter from time to time. It is quite distinctive and is easily recognized as a Cardinal trait after it is heard a few times.

The nest is made of twigs, leaves and grass and is placed in vines, shrubs or trees, seldom very high above the ground. The female does all the brooding of the 3 or 4 eggs that hatch in about twelve days. The male Cardinal is a good husband and a fond parent, however. He feeds the female while she is on the nest and he takes entire care of the feeding of the young when they have left the nest and the female is going about the business of laying more eggs to rear another brood. Sometimes the parent birds bring up three broods in a year.

There was a time when Cardinals were trapped in large numbers and sold as cage birds, but restrictive laws put an end to that trade.

SCARLET TANAGER
(About 7 inches)

You will know the Scarlet Tanager as soon as you set eyes on it. That is, if it's a male in its best dress—a flaming scarlet body with black wings and tail. But the female is easily overlooked. It is nothing like its gorgeous mate. It is an olive-green bird with darker wings and tail. Even the gaudy male takes on the sober olive-green traveling costume when it is time to go southward in the Autumn. It is a curious-looking bird when it is changing from its scarlet coat to its traveling suit. At such times it often looks like a greenish bird that had been spattered with red paint. The young birds of the year are olive-greenish, much like the female. The Scarlet Tanager is a woodland bird but it also likes shade trees on lawns and often will call or sing from an exposed perch on a dead branch. The easiest way to find Scarlet Tanagers is to get to know the song and the call note. They are persistent singers through Spring and Summer. The song is a vibrant continuing warble something like that of the Red-eyed Vireo but with more of metallic buzz in its quality. The call is a snappy "Chip-churrr!" that can be heard at a distance. Once you know the song or the call notes you will be able to find any Scarlet Tanagers that happen to live in your neighborhood—and probably there are more than you suspect. The Scarlet Tanager is a Summer resident over most of the United States east of the Great Plains.

BLUEBIRD
(About 7 inches)

Here is a beautiful, friendly, modest bird with a lovely liquid note and a plaintive song. It has the blue of the sky on its back, the warm color of a hearth fire on its breast and the clear white of soft snow underneath. Whether it is perched on a dead limb or dreamily floating through the air, it keeps up a soft warble all through the day. James Whitcomb Riley, describing the arrival of the first Bluebird of Spring, wrote:

> *In acrost the orchard come,*
> *Soft as an angel's wing,*
> *A breezy, treesy, beesy hum,*
> *Too sweet for any thing!*

Others say that it warbles "Ber-muda, Ber-muda" as it flies daintily over our fields and along the roadsides. It is definitely a bird of the open country and likes to build its nest in bird boxes or holes in fence posts or dead trees around dooryards or barnyards. It is gradually being pushed out of city parks and suburban areas by such imported interlopers as the English Sparrow and the Starling that also nest in holes.

[18]

MOCKINGBIRD
(About 10 inches)

This is the favorite bird of the South, famous in song and story. Like the Nightingale of Europe, the Mockingbird is a plain bird with a beautiful song. It is a generally grayish bird about the size of a Robin, except that it is thinner. When it flies it shows flashes of black and white in its wings and tail. Sitting on a wire, a fence or the branch of a bush or tree, it looks much like its cousin the Catbird but is much lighter in color. The only other bird with which a Mockingbird might be confused is a Shrike. The Loggerhead Shrike is also a grayish bird slightly smaller than the Mockingbird and it is common in many places where the Mockingbird is found, but the Shrike is a chunkier bird with a heavy bill and a black line through the eye. And no Shrike can sing like a Mockingbird. As soon as the singing starts, the Mockingbird never could be mistaken for a Shrike or a Shrike for a Mockingbird.

It is not only the lovely liquid quality but the variations in the Mockingbird's song that make it enchanting. It sings readily by moonlight, too, which adds to the charm. It also is wonderful as a mimic. It can imitate the songs of all the birds of the neighborhood. It can bark like a dog, meow like a cat, creak like a dry wheel and whistle like a postman. It is a bird of inhabited areas. It likes company. You will not find it in the deep woods but around towns and villages and farms. It likes to live near people and pour out melody where it can be heard and enjoyed by human neighbors. Or, at least, it seems that way. It can sing from a perch or sing on the wing. Sometimes it will flutter up from a perch and scatter melody in musical droplets all over the ground beneath.

No wonder the poets and storytellers have done honor to the Mockingbird. It can sing its own song or the song of any other bird it hears. It sings by sunlight or moonlight. It can give a concert from a perch like a tenor singing from a stage, or it can flutter through the air and let a shower of music fall over the landscape. Not only that, but it sings through almost the entire year! The Mockingbird is courageous and in the breeding season is fearless in attacking cats or other raiders that may seem to be threatening its young in the nest. It is bold with other birds and tolerates no impudence from upstarts at the feeding tray or the bird bath. The Mockingbird demands first place there and takes vigorous measures if there is any dispute about it. Though it does eat some cultivated fruit, the Mockingbird is beneficial around the farm or garden because of the great number of injurious insects that it eats.

The nest may be placed anywhere in vines or shrubbery or trees from just off the ground to a branch 50 feet up. There are usually from 3 to 6 eggs and two or even three broods may be raised in a year. Mockingbirds are common over the southern section of the United States east of the Great Plains and may range as far north as eastern Canada.

SONG SPARROW

(About 6 inches)

There are many kinds of Sparrows in all corners of this country and almost all of them are rather plain brownish birds with or without streaked breasts. But if you will look a little closer and also listen to the different songs of the common species, you will easily come to know at least a dozen different kinds. The Song Sparrow, for instance, is found all over North America pouring out its cheerful song that sounds something like "Tea-tea-tea! Polly-put-the-kettle-on!" It is a friendly bird of dooryards, roadsides and open country generally. It varies slightly in color and song in different sections of the country but it can be known by its confident rattling little song and three spots in a triangle on its streaked throat and breast. There are other Sparrows that are brownish above and streaked on the breast, but the Song Sparrow has a dark spot on each side of its throat and a heavy spot in the middle of its breast where the streaks seem to meet in a bunch. Most Song Sparrows go South for the Winter, but a few remain all year in northern territory where snow blankets the ground.

MEADOWLARK

(About 10 inches)

True to its name, the Meadowlark is a bird of the open fields with a clear whistle for a song. It is a stumpy gray-brown bird with a bright yellow breast that has a black crescent across it. It has a striped head and its tail is white on either side, which is a fine mark as the bird flies away when flushed from the grass. The Flicker also has a black crescent on its breast, often feeds on the ground and also shows white on its back as it flies away. But the Flicker's breast is pinkish-brown instead of bright yellow and the white spot it shows flying away is a single patch on its rump. The two white patches that show in the tail of a departing Meadowlark are separated by a dark middle line. The Meadowlark walks when feeding on the ground. Or perhaps it would be better to say that it waddles. Its eggs are laid in a grass-lined depression on the ground. In fact, the bird rarely leaves the ground except when it is disturbed or when it takes some perch from which to sing. It flies with stiff wings and a fluttering style, alternately sailing and beating its wings quickly. Most Meadowlarks are merely Summer residents with us, but a few may stay over Winter.

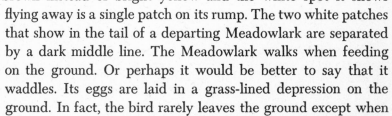

GOLDFINCH

(About 5 inches)

The male Goldfinch in its bright Summer costume is one of the prettiest and daintiest of our native birds, and also one of the easiest to identify with its shining yellow body, its black wings with white bars and its jaunty little black cap pulled down low over its forehead. The female is a much duller color all over and lacks the black cap. These are the birds that many persons call "wild canaries" because they are little yellow birds about canary size and they seem quite friendly as they chatter and twitter when feeding on the lawn or in the garden. They eat seeds for the most part and often come to our lawns for dandelion seeds, which they gobble down with a musical accompaniment. Except in the breeding season, they go about in small groups or flocks, making music as they go. They fly with a long bounding motion, as though they were riding great waves in the air, and at each dip in flight they seem to say "Per-chick-o-ree, Per-chick-o-ree" in musical tones. Their regular and long song is canary-like, a tuneful chattering warble. Even their call notes are musical and sweet. It is easy to know when Goldfinches are in the vicinity because they are rarely silent. They chatter when feeding or resting. Their flight notes come as regularly as their wing movements when they are bounding through the air. They call sweetly to one another all through the day.

There are Goldfinches all over temperate North America and, for the most part, they are permanent residents wherever they are found, though some of them may wander a little in a southerly direction when the Winter winds are at their worst in snow-covered northern territory. The males lose their black caps in Winter and the bright yellow of their Summer plumage turns to the olive-yellow of the female, but the birds lose none of their cheerfulness with this loss of color. They are tuneful and chattering in the dried weed patches of Winter as they are when eating lettuce seeds in the garden in Summer. It is wise to watch the Goldfinch flocks in Winter because these friendly and familiar little birds act as decoys for other and less familiar birds such as Pine Siskins and Redpolls that come down from the more northerly regions to spend some part of the Winter with us.

Goldfinches, Pine Siskins and Redpolls are much alike in shape, size and habits, but the Pine Siskins and the Redpolls are more or less heavily striped and Goldfinches never have stripes. But because even the male Goldfinches are dull of color in Winter, it's wise to inspect any flock of Goldfinches that may be feeding cheerfully on birch cones or weed seeds in Winter. Only a close inspection will show whether or not there are Pine Siskins or Redpolls in with the Goldfinches.

The nest is placed in a fork in an outer branch high up in a tree and it is usually July before the 4 to 6 eggs are laid in a thistledown cradle. Some say the reason for the late nesting is because the female waits for the thistledown to ripen before she builds. The male feeds the female while she is brooding and is a good provider for the young until they leave the nest. Then off they go, parents and young, to join others of their kind and form the tuneful, cheerful, friendly flocks of Goldfinches that are so pleasant to hear and to see.

TOWHEE
(About 8 inches)

This is a bird of many names—Towhee, Chewink, Joe Reed Bird, Ground Robin—the last being a good name for it because the bird sticks close to the ground and often is heard scratching in the underbrush in search of food. There are other Towhees in different parts of the country—the Spotted Towhee and the Green-tailed Towhee of the Far West and Southwest, for instance—but the plain Towhee (or Eastern Towhee, as it is sometimes called) is a common Summer resident over the eastern half of the United States and southern Canada. It ranges as far west as the Great Plains and is the most widespread and best known of the Towhees.

The Towhee is a bird of the underbrush. It lives in thickets, in the bushes that fringe roadsides and along the edges of woods. It is rarely seen on a lawn or on the ground in an open field. It is not common in thick woods. A field that is beginning to grow wild with gray birches, dogwoods, alders and viburnums is a great place for it. It will flit from one bush to the other, showing much white with flirts of its tail as it flies. It will call "Chee-wink, Chee-wink!" from the center of a thicket. Or it may perch atop some shrub or on some limb of a small tree to give its full "Toe-whee" song that is sometimes written "Chuck-burr, pilla-willa."

There is no difficulty in recognizing the Towhee when it does come out of the underbrush or thick shrubbery. Also, it is easy to see why some persons call it the Ground Robin. It does have the dark head of a Robin and it wears something like the red of the Robin's breast on its sides. But the black hood of the Towhee runs well down the breast to meet the clear white of the under parts and the Towhee has much white on the outer edges of its rather long tail. The female and the young have brown where the male Towhee wears black, but the general pattern is the same and the flashing white in the tail as the bird moves about in the underbrush is a sure sign of the Towhee. It almost seems to fly by fits and starts, or in jerks, always with a display of the contrasting colors in its tail. It makes so much noise scratching the leaves aside to find food on the ground that, unless you knew the bird, you might think it was a much larger bird or perhaps some animal at work in there. It feeds on seeds, insects and berries and, on the whole, is considered a beneficial bird.

The Towhee nests on or close to the ground. There are 4 to 6 eggs in a clutch and usually two broods are raised. The second brood frequently comes so late that parents are seen feeding young when it is time for all of them to pack up and be off on the southward migration to avoid the ice and snow of a northern Winter. Sometimes a Towhee will remain through the snows of a northern Winter, but most of our Towhees prefer to move below the Mason-Dixon line when the leaves begin to whirl down with the Autumn winds. If you learn to know this Towhee or the much similar Spotted Towhee of the West, it will be easy to identify other Towhees like the Green-tailed Towhee or the Brown Towhee of the Southwest because of a family likeness in appearance and habits.

RED-WINGED BLACKBIRD
(About 8½ inches)

Here's another common bird that is easy to know. All you have to do is to go to a swamp or marsh and look for a black bird with "red wings". Actually only a small part of the wing is red, but it is enough to identify the bird and give it the name it bears. The bright color is really a shoulder-patch and if you look closely you will see that it is a two-color patch on the grown males. There is an area of deep orange-red fringed by a band of yellowish-red or buff. Anyway, the bright patch stands out against the general black plumage of the male, especially when it is flying or when, from a perch on a cattail or buttonbush, it half-spreads its wings as it gives its cheerful and challenging Spring song of "Kon-keree!" The females and young are dusky striped birds and the gaudy male himself loses much of his lustre in Winter, but the red shoulder-patch always shows when the bird flies. The nest is usually a few feet above water in a low bush, reeds or patch of grass. Some Red-wings stay in the North all year but most of them go South in the Winter.

FLICKER
(About 13 inches)

This is a common bird of many different local names: Flicker, High-hole, Yellow-hammer, Golden-winged Woodpecker, Yaffle, Wicky-up and more. It is a Summer resident over much of North America and one that can hardly escape notice if you keep your eyes and ears open outdoors because it is a good-sized bird of bright colors, is often on the

move over cleared ground and utters loud cries from time to time, including the piercing "flickering" call from which it derives its official name. It's an odd as well as a beautiful bird. It's a woodpecker that spends most of its time on the ground, largely for the purpose of eating ants. Often it flies up from the grass and goes off in strong bounding flight, showing the "gold" in its wings and a good-sized patch of white on its rump. The Flicker is a rich tan-brown in general color, with a small red patch at the back of its head and a black crescent on its breast. It also has dark cross-streaks on its back and many black spots on its underparts. It has a variety of loud and repeated calls that give notice of its presence in any neighborhood. It nests in a hole in a tree and if one is on the nest and you knock on the tree below, the Flicker will stick its head out of the hole to see who is "knocking at the door".

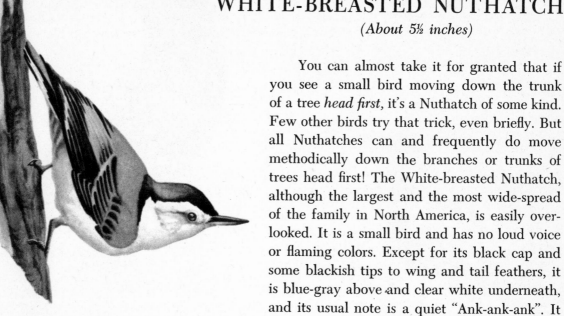

WHITE-BREASTED NUTHATCH
(About 5½ inches)

You can almost take it for granted that if you see a small bird moving down the trunk of a tree *head first,* it's a Nuthatch of some kind. Few other birds try that trick, even briefly. But all Nuthatches can and frequently do move methodically down the branches or trunks of trees head first! The White-breasted Nuthatch, although the largest and the most wide-spread of the family in North America, is easily overlooked. It is a small bird and has no loud voice or flaming colors. Except for its black cap and some blackish tips to wing and tail feathers, it is blue-gray above and clear white underneath, and its usual note is a quiet "Ank-ank-ank". It will eat nuts and seeds but it lives largely on insects that it finds in the bark of trees. It often travels in company with Downy Woodpeckers and Black-capped Chickadees and, being a permanent resident even in cold regions, it will join with them in eating suet if you tie it to a dooryard tree in Winter. Once you have come to know the White-breasted Nuthatch, you will soon learn to know the Red-breasted, the Brown-headed or the Pygmy Nuthatch, depending upon where you live in the United States or Canada.

BLACK-CAPPED CHICKADEE
(About 5 inches)

It's too bad that all birds aren't as polite as the Black-capped Chickadee that identifies itself by saying cheerfully "Chickadee-chickadee-chickadee-dee-dee". It has another "peto" call or song but it's the "chickadee" or simply "dee-de-dee" that is most frequently heard as the little bird bustles about its business of dining on small seeds, insects and insect eggs that it finds in the bark or on the twigs and leaves of shrubs and trees. There are other small  birds of black and white pattern but this one you will know by its black bib as well as its black cap, the bib being tucked neatly under its chin where a good bib should be placed. It travels in groups except in the nesting season and the group is often escorted by one or more Downy Woodpeckers or White-breasted Nuthatches. The Chickadee is a permanent resident over most of North America and is common around dooryards and farmlands in Winter, but it retreats to the woods in the warm months where it nests in holes in trees. If you put out suet or peanuts or sunflower seeds—or even a hard crust of bread—in Winter, you will not have to wait long for a grateful group of Chickadees to come to dine regularly.

BOBOLINK
(About 7 inches)

For a good description of the male Bobolink we can turn to William Cullen Bryant and a poem that many children learn in school:

Robert of Lincoln is gayly dressed,
* Wearing a bright black wedding coat;*
White are his shoulders and white his crest,
* Hear him call in his merry note:*
*   Bob-o-link, bob-o-link,*
*   Spink, spank, spink;*
Look what a nice new coat is mine,
Sure there was never a bird so fine.
*   Chee, chee, chee.*

Robert of Lincoln's Quaker wife,
* Pretty and quiet, with plain brown wings,*
Passing at home a patient life,
* Broods in the grass while her husband sings:*
*   Bob-o-link, bob-o-link,*
*   Spink, spank, spink;*
Brood, kind creature; you need not fear
Thieves and robbers while I am here.
*   Chee, chee, chee.*

The Bobolink, which is a Summer resident of the lush meadows of hay or clover over most of the United States and southern Canada, differs from most birds in that it wears its brightest colors on its back. There are many birds that are dark in color above and clear white below, but the bubbling Bobolink is just the opposite; black below and white— in good part—above. It has a variety of liquid call notes and it pours out a perfect shower of bubbling melody as it flutters upward from the grass in which is hidden its "plain brown wife" on the nest of speckled eggs. The "white cloak" of the handsome male is thrown over its shoulders and down its back in swaggering fashion, but the patch that begins at the back of the head and runs down the neck is a rich cream buff. In late Summer the male changes this "wedding garment" for the streaked yellow-brown costume of the female and young of the year. Then there is a great gathering of the Bobolink clan and they begin the long Autumn migration to Brazil and the Argentine where they spend the Winter. On this 8,000-mile journey all they utter is a metallic "chink" that is, however, so distinctive that, once you know it, you can tell on clear Autumn nights that Bobolinks are on their way to the pampas of South America by the scattered "chinks" that drop down through darkness. Or you may hear the "chinks" by day and catch sight of the Bobolinks high overhead, hurrying southward. But back they come to our meadows in May and once again Robert of Lincoln, quivering with joy, flutters aloft in the sunlight and pours the bubbling melody of his love song over the green grassland that is to be the Summer home of a happy family of Bobolinks.

GRACKLE
(About 12½ inches)

Roughly speaking, Grackles are large Blackbirds with extra long tails. Through all but the coldest months of the year they are spread over most of central and eastern North America in large numbers that are often grouped in great noisy flocks. The experts say there are two species of Grackle that confuse the ordinary observer; the Purple and the Bronzed Grackle. They are approximately the same size. They look much alike. They are difficult to tell apart except when seen fairly close up and in a good light. Their ranges overlap and the species interbreed, producing offspring that even the experts often have trouble classifying.

Let us solve this difficulty by calling these birds—both species—just Grackle. The common (Purple or Bronze) Grackle has a long diamond-shaped tail, much broader in the middle than at either end. That's how you will know the Grackle when you see it walking around on the ground in company with other blackish birds such as Starlings, Cowbirds, Rusty Blackbirds and Red-winged Blackbirds. The Grackles will be noticeably larger than any of these others and, in the sunlight, will have more of a sheen on their plumage. They may be a shining purple around the head and shoulders or the whole back may be a shimmering bronze color. But at any time and in any light, their long tails will make it plain that they are Grackles. Sometimes these tails may be V-shaped, with a "crease" down the center. It is said that the males in Spring "crease" their tails as part of the display in courting the female.

The voice of the Grackle sounds like the name. It's a cross between a creaky "chuck" and a prolonged loud crackle. Except when nesting, they go around in flocks and flood a neighborhood from ground level to treetop, and when hundreds of these birds descend on a lawn or an open field to feed, the din is deafening. They will eat almost anything, including the eggs and young of smaller birds. They do some good by eating harmful insects but they are so numerous in many localities that they are regarded as annoyances if not downright pests. There may be thousands of birds in a single flock in Autumn when the Grackles get together before their southward migration. The migration merely consists in a movement of the birds from southern Canada and the northern part of the United States to the warmer area below the Mason-Dixon line. Some few birds may remain in the North through the Winter but on the whole they do not like snow and ice. As the snow disappears in Spring, the Grackles move northward again and take possession of the country. They like to nest in a pine tree and fairly high above the ground. There are 4 to 6 eggs in a clutch and one brood a year is the rule.

In addition to these common Grackles there is the Boat-tailed Grackle of the Southeast and the Great-tailed Grackle of the Southwest. They are much larger birds with deeply V-shaped tails and there is no danger of confusing them with the ordinary Grackles that are spread so widely and so noisily over this country.

CHIMNEY SWIFT
(About 5½ inches)

The Chimney Swift, wheeling in chattering flight overhead, looks almost exactly like a flying cigar because the body is shaped like a short, fat cigar, the tail is so small that it barely shows, and the wings beat so quickly and so stiffly that the bird seems to be a mechanical thing rather than a living creature. But this little soot-colored bird that prefers to build its nest in chimneys is very much alive and is called a Swift because that's just what it is on the wing—swift! It feeds on the wing, drinks on the wing and even bathes on the wing, dipping down to the surface of the water in full flight. Swifts are insect eaters and their mouths open almost to the full width of their blunt little heads as they sweep through the air, snapping up insects at every turn. They are most active in the evenings and in cloudy weather but they may be seen feeding at almost any time of day. They make a cup-shaped nest of tiny twigs glued with their own saliva to the inside of a chimney. They are Summer residents with us and spend the Winter in Central America.

BARN SWALLOW
(About 7 inches)

Probably the most abundant, the most familiar and the most beautiful of our native Swallows is the Barn Swallow. It is truly a deserted farm building that doesn't have a Barn Swallow's nest in it. Under the eaves, along the beams, or high up on an inner wall of barn, silo, ice house, woodshed or wagon house, these birds plaster their nests of mud and grass, lay their 3 to 6 eggs and rear their young. The only other native swallow with which it might be confused is the Cliff Swallow, but from the Cliff Swallow as well as all others it may be known by its deeply forked tail with the spines of the two outer feathers sticking out like stiff wires. All Swallows are insect eaters, catching their prey on the wing in the chattering, sweeping, graceful flight with which we all are familiar. There are many species in this country, all of them beneficial and beautiful birds. When you know the Barn Swallow, you can begin to know the others by watching to see how the less familiar ones differ from the lovely Barn Swallow that is always on the wing around our farmyards in the Summer. They raise two broods with us and then fly off swiftly to spend the Winter in South America.

PHOEBE

(About 7 inches)

The Phoebe is probably the most common Flycatcher over the eastern half of North America. Flycatchers—and there are numerous species in different parts of the country—usually dart from a perch to snap up insects in the air and then return to a perch, often the same perch from which they started. It is frequently difficult to know one Flycatcher from another because of similarity in size, color and general markings, but happily their songs or call notes are quite different and the Phoebe is among those easy to identify by voice. Its regular and frequently repeated double note is "Phee-bee, phee-bee," from which it derives its name. It is a small bird that is grayish-brown above, growing darker on the head, and white underneath. It has the habit of wagging its tail while perched. It likes to build in and around houses, barns and farm buildings of any kind. Any projection under cover will do as a support for its nest. It has no eye ring or wing bars or outstanding mark of any kind. It is dull-colored but friendly and, if you are in doubt about its identity, it will speak up and name itself.

KINGBIRD

(Nearly 9 inches)

The flashing Kingbird is one of the larger and more noisy members of the Flycatcher family. It is dark gray above, clear white underneath and it has a white band across the tip of its tail. This band is quite easy to spot as the bird flies overhead in pursuit of insects or for the purpose of heckling the larger birds of the neighborhood, a habit that gives the Kingbird its common name. It perches on the topmost limb of small trees and launches

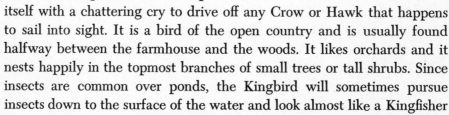

itself with a chattering cry to drive off any Crow or Hawk that happens to sail into sight. It is a bird of the open country and is usually found halfway between the farmhouse and the woods. It likes orchards and it nests happily in the topmost branches of small trees or tall shrubs. Since insects are common over ponds, the Kingbird will sometimes pursue insects down to the surface of the water and look almost like a Kingfisher plunging for fish. Like the other Flycatchers, it heads southward in Autumn. The Kingbird is alert and courageous and if you see a small bird impudently making passes at a Hawk and uttering shrill cries, it probably will be a Kingbird.

BELTED KINGFISHER

(About 13 inches)

The Belted Kingfisher is a good-sized blue and white bird that flies along ponds, streams, rivers and lakes with a rattling cry and occasionally dives headlong into the water in pursuit of some small fish. If it is successful in its plunge, you will see the fish in its bill when the Kingfisher comes up and you will hear a rattle of triumph as the bird flies off with its prey. The Kingfisher is larger than a Robin and has a rough dark crest that sticks up like hair that the bird neglected to comb. The male is blue-gray above and clear white underneath except for a broad band of blue-gray that runs from the bird's shoulders across its breast. The female is the same except for an extra chestnut-rufous band that runs below the blue-gray band across its breast and down its flanks. Kingfishers are odd birds in that the female has more color than the male and they are odd in another way, too. They nest in holes in banks, either along water or as near water as possible. The birds tunnel into the banks—sometimes a distance of ten feet or more—and lay their 5 to 8 eggs at the inner ends of the tunnels. Kingfishers are common residents all over North America and will spend the Winter as far north as they can find open water on ponds, lakes and rivers.

The only other bird with which the Kingfisher might be confused is the Blue Jay and there are decided differences, beginning with the bill, which is conspicuously long and heavy in the Kingfisher. The Blue Jay has a neat crest, white wing bars, a flashy tail and graceful lines. The Kingfisher has a raggedy crest, no wing bars, a short tail, short legs and a generally chunky or stubby appearance. The Kingfisher is almost invariably found perched above or flying along a body of water, whereas the Blue Jay is a bird of hill and dale, of suburban lawns, of the open fields and the wooded hillsides.

There is a lovely Greek legend about the origin of Kingfishers. The story is that beautiful Halcyone, daughter of Aeolus, King of the Winds, married the young and handsome Ceyx, King of Trachinia, and that Ceyx shortly thereafter went on a voyage and was drowned. Not knowing this and longing for the return of her husband, Halcyone walked the seashore each day until one morning the waves washed her husband's body to her feet. She was so overcome with sorrow that she threw herself into the sea. But as she did so she and her dead husband were changed into Kingfishers and flew off happily together. Now we refer to bright sunlit days on the water as "halcyon days" because of a Greek legend.

COWBIRD

(About 8 inches)

There are many persons who insist that the Cowbird is a villain but the first thing to do is to identify the alleged culprit and then take up the case of the crime charged against it. The Cowbird is the smallest of our native Blackbirds. The male is a shining black except for its head, which is a rich brown when seen in a good light. The female and young are gray-brown, just about the size and somewhat the same color as female and young Starlings but there is little difficulty in telling them apart. The Starlings are chunkier birds with long bills and short tails. The Cowbirds have short conical bills like English Sparrows, are slimmer than Starlings and have what you might call a tail of standard size. Female and young Redwinged Blackbirds are dark brown but they are heavily streaked, so there is no danger of confusing them with the unstreaked female or young Cowbirds. Where mixed Blackbirds are walking about in flocks and feeding together, the Cowbirds will be the smaller, roundheaded, short-billed birds at all times. The Cowbird has a pleasantly liquid "glug-glug" call note but the Spring song of the male is a most ridiculous performance, a rasping gurgle delivered with swelling throat and half-spread wings and tail as though the bird were choking in agony. It's a combination of bubbles and squeaks on a sliding scale and anything but musical.

Now we come to the high crime charged against the Cowbird, which is that they never build nests of their own but foist their offspring on other birds. Like the European Cuckoo, the female Cowbird sneaks through trees and shrubbery until she finds a suitable nest with eggs in it and the owner absent. Then the female Cowbird deposits an egg in the nest and hurriedly departs, leaving the egg to be hatched and the young bird to be reared by the real owner of the nest, usually a smaller bird than the Cowbird. Thus the young Cowbird, at hatching or shortly thereafter, is the biggest and strongest of the youngsters and soon overwhelms the other young birds in the nest. It is a rare thing for any young except the Cowbird fledgling to survive in a group like this. It is almost certain that every Cowbird that you see was hatched and reared at the cost of a whole brood of some smaller bird and it is astonishing what a wide variety of victims the female Cowbird picks out when she goes about laying eggs. It is said that more than a hundred different kinds of birds have been swindled in this manner by the Cowbird but their favorite victims seem to be the Warbler family, Phoebes, Song Sparrows and Red-eye Vireos. Sometimes the real owner of the nest will discover the swindle and do something about it. Robins have been known to notice the Cowbird eggs in their nests and destroy them. Yellow Warblers sometimes note the strange egg with their own, abandon the whole clutch, and build another nest atop the first one in which to lay other eggs. But, alas, sometimes the Cowbird comes around to lay another foreign egg in the second-story nest, too. Or even a third-story nest.

RED-EYED VIREO

(About 6 inches)

The Vireos in North America are a group of about a dozen species of small and, for the most part, greenish-yellow birds that are seen going over the branches, twigs and leaves of shrubs and trees in more or less deliberate and methodical search for insects. They are not colorful or fluttery birds. The Yellow-throated Vireo is a bird of the upper branches of trees and the White-eyed Vireo is a haunter of the thickets, hedgerows and alder swamps, but the abundant and cheerful Red-eyed Vireo hunts high and low by hill and dale all over the United States and southern Canada, moving steadily along the branches and among the leaves of shrubs and trees and singing a pleasant but slightly monotonous song all the while. It seems to be saying "I see you—you see me—I see you—so what?" The Red-eyed Vireo is more greenish than yellow above, clear white below, and has a darkish gray cap beneath which is a white eye stripe outlined in black above. The deliberate movements, the gray cap of this greenish bird and its persistent song through the Summer are the best marks by which to identify it. Once you have come to know the Red-eyed Vireo, it will be easier for you to make the acquaintance of the other and less familiar and abundant members of the family.

WOOD THRUSH

(About 8 inches)

This is probably the most abundant and the most familiar of our Thrushes—except the Robin and the Bluebird, which are members of the Thrush family—east of the Mississippi River. Like most members of the family, this is a bird of the woodlands and a beautiful singer. But the Wood Thrush is a little more friendly than some of its shy relatives and often inhabits suburban lawns and builds its nest in cultivated shrubbery or shade trees. It is smaller than a Robin, generally brownish above and white beneath, with a heavily spotted breast. Viewed close up, the bright reddish-brown of its head gradually fades into the olive-brown of its tail. Some of the brownish Thrushes are difficult to tell apart but the heavy dots on the white breast of the Wood Thrush are a good mark, as is the reddish head. Since it often comes on lawns and readily takes to a bird bath, it is easier to have a good view of it than of the more timid wood-haunting species. Finally there is the song, which is lovely and liquid, a two-part song that is repeated again and again.

[31]

HERMIT THRUSH
(*About 7 inches*)

You have to go to the woods to see or hear this bird, and the chances are that you will hear it before you see it. In fact, you may have a hard time finding it even when you hear it, because it is a shy bird that keeps flitting away through the trees and the undergrowth when intruders appear in its shady domain. We have in temperate North America some seven brownish-backed Thrushes with spotted breasts and it isn't always easy to know them apart. It takes time to discover the little differences among them in color, spotting and shading. And it may take some traveling, too, because the Olive-backed Thrush of the East is practically the same bird as the Russet-backed Thrush of the West, just as the Willow Thrush of the West is merely a distant twin of the eastern Veery.

The Veery is the reddish-backed Thrush with little spotting on its breast and a rippling, ringing song that spirals downward. Its haunt is the low wet woods or the shadier part of a swamp. The Wood Thrush is the one with the large and numerous blackish spots on its breast and a reddish color on its head that fades to brownish-olive toward its tail. The Hermit Thrush shading runs just the opposite way—it is olive-brownish on its head and shades to reddish on the tail. Its breast spots are not as numerous or as large as those of the Wood Thrush, and it has a habit of flicking its tail every now and then when it is perched or standing still on the ground. The Wood Thrush, of course, comes readily to our lawns and nests in our dooryard shrubbery or shade trees. And its clear, sweet but unvaried song beginning "Ee-o-lee" is a definite distinguishing mark even when the singer is unseen. The song of the Hermit Thrush is something else. It has a dream-like quality. It begins gently and floats upward "like clouds of incense ascending". The notes are liquid and delightful with just the hint of a bell tone to some of them. The bird has several phrases and sings in different keys in gentle succession, but it is never the exact same song that the bird sang before. There is just enough variation to give the impression that it is all improvised, a bird pouring out its heart in melody. In the shadier parts of the woods it may be heard singing at any time of day, but most of its singing is done at dawn or in the hush of evening. It is wonderful to hear it in the woods at twilight—a lovely, liquid, dreamy, ethereal song floating upward through the darkening woods.

The Hermit Thrush spends much of its time feeding on the floor of the woods, turning over dead leaves in search of insects or their eggs or grubs. It nests on the ground or close to it. It often ventures out into clearings or along the edge of the woods to build its nest, which usually is made of mosses, grasses and pine needles. There are usually 4 greenish-blue eggs in the cup-shaped nest and there may be two or more broods a season. It is the last of our Thrushes to retreat before oncoming snow when the northern Winter approaches and it is the first of the family to slip northward again in Spring. It has a harsh call note that almost grates on the ear, but it's always good to hear it because, in the woods of Spring and Summer, it means that the Hermit Thrush is there and sooner or later we will enjoy its marvelous melodies.

VEERY
(About 7 inches)

The Veery is a Summer resident of the greater part of North America and a persistently vocal one in a nice way. It is easily found and easily recognized. It is the reddest or, at least, the tawniest of our brownish-backed Thrushes with spotted breasts. It has fewer and lighter spots on its breast than the others in the group. It is the most water-loving of the family. It loves swamps or low wet woods or even wet meadows that are beginning to be overrun by alders, willows, gray birches and viburnums. It has a lyrical, rippling, circling song that spirals downward and easily marks it apart from any of its group except the Willow Thrush of the West. Anything that is said of the Veery or its song might just as well apply to the Willow Thrush. Only the expert ornithologist would know one of these birds from the other by the slight difference in shading. To the ordinary observer the only difference is that the Veery is found over the central and eastern half of the country and the Willow Thrush is a Summer resident of the Northwest. For convenience, here we can stick to the Veery. It is far more widespread over the country. To find the Veery, go to the edge of any swamp from May to July and listen. Soon you will hear a flute-like rippling series of notes that begin high and spiral downward. That will be the Veery. But seeing the bird may be more difficult, and may take some time.

MAGPIE
(About 20 inches)

There never is any question about the identity of a Magpie if you see one. There is no other bird like it, except another species of Magpie. In this case our bird is the common Black-billed or American Magpie that may be found anywhere from Texas to Alaska in a broad belt of country extending from the foothills of the Rockies as far east as Kansas and Nebraska. There is another smaller species, the Yellow-billed Magpie, that is found in the valleys of central California. But wherever they are found, Magpies are large and conspicuous birds with glistening black heads, much black and white on wings and body, and enormous tails that stream out behind them when they fly. Except in the breeding season, they travel about in flocks like Crows, to whom they are related, but they are bolder than Crows when it comes to descending upon barnyards and dooryards and kitchen gardens. The Magpie has all the curiosity, impudence and knavish tricks of the Blue Jay—another of its relatives, by the way—and will steal practically anything it can carry off. It makes a huge nest of mud and twigs that is roofed over and entered from the sides. The nest is usually placed in a thorn bush to make it hard for any enemy to get near it. Magpies are regarded as permanent residents over much of their range but some of the more northerly residents may take southern trips in Winter.

WHITE-CROWNED SPARROW

(About 7 inches)

Many persons never bother to look at Sparrows, thinking that they are all little brownish birds of no particular distinction. The truth is that we have a wonderful assortment of Sparrows in North America and many of them are useful, handsome and melodious birds. They are small, to be sure. And most of them are brownish above and lighter below, with or without streaks on their breasts. But if you look closely you will see that there are many Sparrows in your neighborhood that differ very much in their markings, and if you hear them sing you will immediately note the wide differences in their songs. The White-Crowned Sparrow, which is found all over temperate North America either as a Summer resident or a seasonal migrant, is a really handsome bird with an aristocratic air about it. It is much more common in the West than it is in the East. There are slight differences in some of their markings and the experts divide them into "races" with added names such as "Gambel's Sparrow" and "Nuttall's Sparrow", but this need not concern beginners.

WHITE-THROATED SPARROW

(About 6¾ inches)

This is the only bird that might be confused with the White-crowned Sparrow because it is almost the same size and has its head similarly marked with brilliant black and white stripes, but the White-throated Sparrow is well named and its white bib tucked under its chin stands out clearly against the rather dull gray of its breast. Furthermore, the White-throated Sparrow has a yellow spot where the white eye-line runs into the bill. The yellow spot is brighter in Spring than in the Fall but at almost any time of year there is enough yellow there to be noticeable. The adult "White-throats", as they are commonly called, have unstreaked gray breasts like the slightly larger White-crowned Sparrows, but young "White-throats" generally have obscure streakings on the breast and flanks in the Autumn. The White-throated Sparrow is much more common in the eastern part of North America than the White-crowned Sparrow. It is known in some regions as the "Peabody bird" because of its song in which it is supposed to say: "Old Sam Peabody, Peabody, Peabody". Like the White-crowned Sparrow, it breeds in Canada and the higher ground of the northern United States, and is a common roadside bird on migration.

[34]

CHIPPING SPARROW

(About 5¼ inches)

The abundant and friendly little "Chippy", found all over North America in the warmer months, is another of the clear-breasted Sparrows and one of the smallest members of this large family. It wears a dark reddish-chestnut cap below which is a clear white line fringed along the lower edge by a thinner black line running through the eye to the base of the little dark conical bill. Its small size and the clearly marked and neat pattern of its "side face" help to distinguish the Chipping Sparrow from some of the other small and clear-breasted Sparrows. Another distinguishing mark is its song (if you can call it that), which is a monotonous succession of metallic-sounding "chips" strung together so rapidly that it almost amounts to a trill. The Chipping Sparrow usually is seen on the ground but often it goes aloft to a perch to deliver this song. It certainly isn't musical but it is a loud song for such a small bird.

The Chipping Sparrow is a familiar dooryard denizen all across the country. It hops about lawns, feeding on grass seed and weed seed. It also gobbles up many insects "in season" and is said to be an efficient destroyer of gipsy moths, canker worms, grasshoppers and weevils. On migration the Chipping Sparrow may be found almost anywhere but in the breeding season it makes itself at home on open ground and cleared land. It is not usually found in the woods or even in meadows where the grass is thick and high. It likes pasture lands that cattle have grazed close and it will be found along the roadsides and around barnyards and gardens. But most of all it likes a well-kept lawn and the company of human beings. It builds readily in dooryards, often in vines climbing over porches. It places its neat but frail nests anywhere from just off the ground to fairly high in a tree and the little cradle of woven grasses is usually lined with hair from a horse's tail. With tractors replacing horses on so many farms, the Chipping Sparrow may soon encounter a shortage of building material. There are 3 to 5 eggs in a clutch and there may be one or two broods a season. The female does most of the brooding of the eggs while the male does the foraging and brings food to the female on the nest.

The Cowbird finds the Chipping Sparrow an easy victim of its trick of depositing a Cowbird egg in another nest and letting a foster-parent hatch and rear the Cowbird youngster. It's funny to see a little Chipping Sparrow feeding a much larger clamoring young Cowbird in July or August. But the Chipping Sparrow is no exception among small birds in that way. It is always interesting when young Cowbirds are heard squealing in Summer to wait around to find out just what kind of bird has been victimized. The assortment of victims is astonishing.

As soon as cold weather creeps over Canada and the northern section of the United States, the Chipping Sparrows of that region begin a retreat toward the South. There is a concentration of these birds below the Mason-Dixon Line in Winter and they are in no particular hurry to go back north again, either. It isn't until warm weather has really arrived "up North" that the Chipping Sparrow will be found back on the front lawn again in our Northern States and Canada.

[35]

SLATE-COLORED JUNCO
(About 6¼ inches)

Look for the Junco in cold weather. It is a bird of the North and for most of us it is a Winter visitor to our dooryards. It breeds in Canada and on high ground in our Northern States. On its breeding range it is a bird of lonely pastures, of cool woods, of stark country where tree growth is stunted and barren ground stretches away toward the Arctic Circle. But about the time of the first frost, the Juncos come drifting down daintily all over the United States and remain with us until the call of Spring sends them back to their breeding range again. Many persons call them "Snowbirds", which is a good name for them because they come to us for the colder months, are common sights around a snow-covered dooryard and, with much white in their plumage, are as light as snowflakes on the wing.

There are half a dozen species of Junco to be found at some season in some parts of the United States but the Slate-colored Junco is by all odds the most abundant and the most widespread over the United States and Canada in general. Once you learn to know the Slate-colored Junco, you can keep your eyes open for the other species, especially if you live in the West where they are more frequently to be found. In the East, any Junco except a Slate-colored Junco is a rarity. It is well-named, being slate-colored above and a soft grayish-white below, but the mark that most easily catches the eye is the flashing of the white outer tail feathers as the bird flits away from the observer. The bird also has a light-colored bill and a characteristic "tsip" that sometimes is extended into a weak buzz or trill as it feeds or flits about the shrubbery, but look for a little dark gray bird that goes off in short flights with a display of white outer tail feathers and that will be the Junco.

Often a flock of Juncos will start scattering and flitting away almost from under your feet, for they are not particularly shy and they spend most of their time on the ground, feeding in our dooryards, our barnyards, our shorn harvest fields and the weed patches in neglected corners. They flood the country roadsides and every passing person or vehicle sets them flitting along the ground with a great display of white outer tail feathers. They are found in the woods, too. In fact, Juncos are everywhere in Winter and nowhere in Summer—or, at least, not where most of us can see them. To find the Junco on its breeding range we would have to go to Canada or the cool woodlands of the high ground of our Northern States. There in Summer we might hear the song of the Slate-colored Junco, a monotonous trill somewhat like and not much more musical than the "song" of the Chipping Sparrow, and there on or a little above the ground we might find the nest of the "Snowbird" with 4 to 6 eggs in it any time from May to July. But if you can't visit its breeding grounds, just wait for Autumn and with the falling of the leaves, the Junco will be back in your dooryard. If you put out seeds and water for them, they will be regular visitors at your feeding station. Cold weather and snow never seem to bother them at all, and they are cheerful and delightful visitors to have for the Winter.

CACTUS WREN
(About 8 inches)

Those who know Wrens in other parts of the country will be surprised if they ever come upon the Cactus Wren of the Southwest. It is the giant of the Wren family in this country and so shaped and marked that it looks more like a small Thrasher than it does a large Wren. But it is a true Wren that may be found almost anywhere in the cactus country pouring out its rackety-rax song all day and, for that matter, almost all year. It perches atop some cactus plant where it can be easily seen when singing. It is a brown color above and white below, with many numerous heavy spots on its throat and breast. It has a clearly defined white eye-line and it shows much white spotting in its outer tail feathers when it flies. It is famous for its large round nest with a tunnel entrance that it builds of plant fibers and lines with bird feathers. It is usually placed in a cactus plant in such a way that the thorns defy marauders to attack the premises. Not all the nests have eggs in them. There are extra nests that perhaps are built as decoys. It is said that, after the breeding season, Cactus Wrens may take refuge in these nests during rainstorms or spells of cold, windy weather.

BROWN CREEPER
(About 5½ inches)

This is one of the easiest birds to overlook. It is about the size and general color of a small Sparrow—brown on its back and white underneath—but it doesn't act or live like any of the Sparrows. It is rarely if ever seen on the ground. It goes about with Chickadees, Woodpeckers and Nuthatches. and makes a living the way they do. It creeps up tree trunks, often in a spiral, beginning at the base of the tree and winding its way up out of sight. It searches for insects, insect eggs and larva in the crevices of the bark. When it has worked its way as high up as it cares to go on one tree, it drops off and flies down to the base of another tree to work its way up again. It clings so close to the tree and goes over the bark so thoroughly that it looks almost like a brown mouse climbing a tree. It has a beady "screeping" note that it sometimes utters as it winds its way up a tree trunk. We see it mostly in cold weather when it comes around with the Chickadees, Nuthatches and Kinglets—a little brown bird with a curved bill that creeps spirally up the trunks of trees.

MOURNING DOVE
(About 12 inches)

The Mourning Dove, shaped like a small thin Pigeon, is a rich tan-brown in general color, with some black spots on its back, glints of pink, blue and chocolate shading here and there, and a long pointed tail with white showing plainly on the outer feathers as the bird rises from the ground and flies off. It is almost an exact copy of the much larger Passenger Pigeon that once covered this country's skyways in enormous flocks and is now extinct, the victim of almost incredible slaughter by relentless market hunters. There were few or no game laws in many sections of the country when Passenger Pigeons were being shot, trapped, netted or actually clubbed down from tree branches by the millions each year, and the few game laws enacted were rarely enforced. So the Passenger Pigeon was harried to extinction in a land where its great flocks once darkened the skies. Conditions are much different now and though the Mourning Dove is considered a game bird and is much shot at in the hunting season, especially in the South where the flocks are numerous and widespread in Autumn and Winter, it seems to be holding its own across the country.

The Mourning Dove is commonly a ground feeder, walking about like a domestic Pigeon picking up food. It consumes many weed seeds and grass seeds and you will often find Mourning Doves coming to the grain fields for the leavings after the harvesters have come and gone. The birds also come like gleaners to the bare fields of Autumn from which crops of corn, peas, buckwheat and beans have been taken. Often they will be encountered on hard ground or roads surfaced with gravel, picking up the little stones and bits of gravel that are needed in their gizzards to aid digestion. But Mourning Doves often are seen in trees, too, or perched on telephone wires. They are fond of the blue berry of the Sour Gum (or Tupelo, as the tree is called in many sections) and will eat wild berries of various kinds. One of the things that is soon noticed about Mourning Doves is the peculiar noise made by the birds in flying. It has been called a "winnowing sound", for want of any better description. But it will strike any listener almost immediately and it is a sound made by no other bird in flight. Aside from that, the Mourning Dove makes no noise other than its long-drawn, moaning coo that is heard more frequently in the Spring. This is the mournful sound that gives the bird the name of Mourning Dove. On the whole it might be said that the Mourning Dove is one of the most quiet of our birds as the Blue Jay is one of the noisiest.

Sometimes the Mourning Dove will lay its two eggs in a mere depression on the ground but in general it builds a skimpy nest of twigs in a tree or moves into an old nest left by some other bird like the Robin, Brown Thrasher, Mockingbird or Blue Jay. For the first few days the fledglings receive "predigested food" like young Pigeons, reaching into the throats of their fond parents for it, but soon they go on the regular Dove diet of a few worms and berries and many, many seeds and grains.

GOLDEN-CROWNED KINGLET
(About 4 inches)

Kinglets are tiny olive-greenish birds that come to us as Autumn migrants or Winter residents after the Warblers have gone southward, and they leave for cooler regions about the time that the Warblers come back to us in Spring. The Kinglets breed in Canada and high altitudes in the United States. They like to forage in evergreens but they also work over other trees and shrubs and if you see a tiny olive-greenish bird with whitish wing-bars flitting about a bush in Warbler-fashion in cold weather, it probably is a Kinglet. If it has a golden patch running back from its forehead over its head, it will be the Golden-crowned Kinglet. The golden patch is bordered with black and the bird has a distinct white eye-stripe. The Ruby-crowned Kinglet is similar in size, shape and general color, including the wing-bars, but it lacks the golden crown patch and the eye-line. Do not look for any ruby crown by which to identify the Ruby-crowned Kinglet, because that sign is like the red flag on a taximeter; it only goes up when the operator puts it up. The ruby crown is invisible most of the time. It is worn and displayed only by the male on special occasions when it is courting a female or challenging another male. If you see a Kinglet with a golden-crown patch and a distinct eye-line, it must be the Golden-crowned Kinglet. If you see a Kinglet with no crown patch and a side face unmarked except for a tiny white circle around the eye that gives the bird a frightened look, that will be the Ruby-crowned Kinglet. In the Spring before the Kinglets disappear to cooler regions you may—if you are lucky—see the "red flag" of the Ruby-crowned Kinglet and hear its wonderful bubbling song.

BLACK AND WHITE WARBLER
(About 5¼ inches)

Warblers are, for the most part, small and brightly-colored birds of many species that are seen in the United States and Canada as Summer residents or migrants. Many of the species breed in the Canadian forests and winter in Central America or South America and these species are seen in the United States on their migrations to and from their breeding grounds. But there are dozens of species that are Summer residents of the United States and some few species that remain in various sections of the country throughout the year. One of the most widespread of these dainty little birds is the Black and White Warbler, which is sometimes called the Black and White Creeper because of its actions. It does "creep" about the trunks and branches of trees in the manner of the Brown Creeper, but it "creeps" in all directions instead of following the standard upward spiral of the Brown Creeper. There are several other Warblers that are colored black and white—the Blackpoll and the Black-throated Gray Warbler—but those birds have solid black caps whereas this bird's head is streaked.

YELLOW WARBLER
(About 5 inches)

The Yellow Warbler is a Summer resident of practically all of North America to the edge of the Arctic country. It is well named and easily identified, a small bird that seems to be bright yellow all over, for which reason it is often called a "Wild Canary" along with the Goldfinch. But the Goldfinches always have dark wings and tails whereas the Yellow Warbler is completely yellow except that the male has cinnamon-reddish stripes on its under parts. The female has few or no stripes below. Yellow Warblers are found most commonly in rather open country with scattered trees and thickets. They like swamps that include a fair supply of maples, elms, ashes, willows, alders and dogwoods whose leaves and branches they inspect in search of insects on which they dine. The Yellow Warbler has a loud song of the "switch-switch-switchy" type and is one of the most persistent singers of all the Warblers. The female does most of the nest-building, weaving a neat cup-shaped structure of grasses and plant fibers for her 3 to 5 eggs. The nest is usually in some low growth from a foot to ten feet above ground and if the female discovers that a Cowbird has laid an unwanted extra egg in the nest, she may abandon that nest and build another one right on top of it. There is a report of a case where that process was repeated six times; a 6-story Yellow Warbler structure, with a Cowbird's egg in each nest, including the top one! So that attempt to foil the Cowbird was vain.

MYRTLE WARBLER
(About 5½ inches)

The Myrtle Warbler is a blue-gray little bird that, on closer inspection, shows streaks and patches of black, white and shining yellow. The female is duller but most of the distinguishing marks are clear enough to be observed, particularly the yellow rump that is such a mark that the species is sometimes called the Yellow-rumped Warbler. In addition to the yellow on the rump, the Myrtle Warbler has a yellow crown patch and yellow patches on each side of the breast. The bird has a white throat and a black patch across the breast, with the black running down the flanks and breaking up into spots and streaks. It is one of the most abundant Warblers over the central and eastern section of the United States and in the West it is replaced by Audubon's Warbler, which is quite similar in marking except that it has a yellow throat instead of the white throat of the Myrtle Warbler. The bright yellow patches on the crown and breast in Spring plumage may be barely noticeable in the Fall traveling costume but the yellow rump is the identification tag of the bird in any plumage. Myrtle Warblers breed from the Canadian Border area northward to the tree line. They are early arrivals among the Spring migrants, sometimes seeming to fill every bush and tree in the neighborhood.

OVENBIRD
(About 6 inches)

If you go into the woods in May or June you probably will hear from the undergrowth a series of notes sounding something like "teacher-Teacher-TEACHER-TEACHER-TEACHER!", the series rising to a loud climax at the end. If you trace the sound to its source, you will find that it comes from a small olive-greenish bird walking calmly about the ground like a chicken. This is the Ovenbird or Teacher-Bird or Golden-crowned Thrush. It is known by all three names for three good reasons. It is called the Ovenbird because its nest is oven-shaped and the mother bird enters it from the side. It is called the Teacher-Bird because that's what listeners think they hear it saying in emphatic tones. It is called the Golden-crowned Thrush because it looks much like a small Thrush and it has an orange-brown patch running from its forehead back over its crown in the manner of the Golden-crowned Kinglet, except that the Ovenbird's crown is somewhat darker and not so glowing in hue.

The Ovenbird is one of the Warbler family but it is quite unlike most members of that family in appearance and habits. It does not flutter quickly and nervously through the foliage of shrubs and trees in search of its insect food and it is not bright-colored. The general tone of the bird above is olive-greenish except for its orange-brownish crown. Underneath it is white with dark stripes that look like spots placed so close together that they formed streaks. The real mark of distinction about this bird, however, is the solemn way it stalks about the ground while its more brilliant cousins—meaning most of the Warblers—flit through the greenery like so many feathered butterflies. It is almost exclusively a bird of the woods and, except on migration, is rarely encountered in open country. It is a Summer resident of most of the woodlands of central and eastern North America and rather easy to find because of its loud song.

It is much more difficult, however, to locate its curious nest because the Ovenbird takes great pains to hide the structure. It is built on the ground and usually on a slope. It may be at the base of a sapling Hemlock or Juniper or perhaps along the "shoulder" of a wood road. It's a roofed-over structure of grass, bark, plant fibers, dead leaves and other such material and the entrance is on the side so that, when you peer in at the 4 to 6 eggs, it really does seem that they have been tucked away in an oven. If the bird is frightened from the nest, it does not fly off but scurries away like a mouse over the ground.

In September the Ovenbirds begin their Autumn migration southward to Central America and on this trip they are often seen in public parks and patches of shrubbery on suburban lawns, but in the Summer they are birds of the woods and that's where you have to go to see them walking about the forest floors. The only birds with which they might be confused because of similarity in size, shape and habit of walking about the ground in the woods are the Water Thrushes and, if you get a good look, there are differences that are quite easily noted. The Water Thrushes stick fairly close to water; they twitch their tails nervously; they have distinct eye-lines. The Ovenbird has the orange-brown crown patch, no eye-line and may be found anywhere in the woods. But the easiest way is to listen for its "teacher" notes and track down the performer.

REDSTART
(About 5½ inches)

Seen against the light greenery of the Spring woods, the Redstart is like a tiny darting flame. It is a striking combination of black above, white below and flashing patches of brilliant orange-red in its wings and tail. There is also some orange-red on its breasts and flanks but the bright patches in the wings and the tail flare out and catch the eye as the bird flits from one tree or one branchlet to another. It is the most active of our Warblers, forever on the move in quick darts against a green background. The female is much less brilliant. It is rather olive-greenish above where the male is black and its wing, tail, breast and flanks are decorated with yellow where the male wears the brilliant orange-red. The young of the year are like the female and in late Summer and early Autumn, as the birds gather for the southward migration, most of the Redstarts that you will see will be of the less colorful kind, the females and young of the year. But even these females and young attract attention as they flutter about the trees and shrubs because of the yellow patches in their tails. The patches stand out because Redstarts have longish tails for such small birds and they are always spreading them like fans as they dart about in search of insects. But the shining male in Spring is really the Redstart in its glory, a bird of the woods that is as bright as any lily of the field. It is a Summer resident of most of temperate North America and you should be able to find it if you go into the woods and watch for a tiny flash of flame amid the green foliage of the trees.

YELLOWTHROAT
(About 5¼ inches)

This sprightly little bird probably should be called the "Bandit Warbler" because it lurks in the shrubbery and underbrush and pops out suddenly with a black mask over its face. It is olive-greenish above and it shades from a bright yellow on its throat to a pale yellowish wash on the remainder of its under parts, but its attractive and striking feature is the black mask that looks exactly as if the bird had tied it on to take up an outlaw career. The upper edge of the black mask is fringed with a light gray border of varying width in different individuals. The female and young do not have the black mask but the yellow throat that gives them their name is a good guide to their identity. The Yellowthroat is a Summer resident of eastern North America and it likes lowlands that are well watered. It is found in wet meadows, swamps, bushy pastures and roadsides not far from water. It is plentiful along brooks and the fringes of lakes, ponds and rivers. It has a fairly loud chip and a triple-note song that some interpret as "Witchery, witchery, witchery". It is a distinctive song, easily learned, and when you know it you will have no trouble finding Yellowthroats in the thick grasses and the low bushes in May and June.

YELLOW-BREASTED CHAT
(About 7½ inches)

The Chat is an odd bird of striking appearance and astonishing vocal ability. At first glance it might look like an overgrown Yellowthroat because its throat is a brilliant yellow and it is blackish around the face as well as olive-greenish along the remainder of its upper parts. But the blackish tinge running back from the bill a brief distance over the cheeks and crown of the bird is lightened by a white line over the eye, a white circle around the eye and a short white line on each side of its chin. It doesn't have the "masked" look of the Yellowthroat and it is a much larger bird. Furthermore, the Yellowthroat keeps repeating "Witchery, witchery, witchery" to identify itself whereas the Chat gives off an astonishing and bewildering variety of whistles, squeaks, chuckles, bubbles, and squawks. Like the Catbird, Mockingbird, and Starling, it can imitate all the birds of the neighborhood, but the Mockingbird and Starling do it in the open while the Catbird does it from a bush and the Chat usually does it from some hidden nook in a tangle of catbriar. A Chat nearby in a thicket can make a noise like a dog barking at a distance. It is a feathered ventriloquist and it seems to take delight in tricking listeners into looking at the wrong places for the source of those strange sounds. It can caw like a crow, meow like a cat, croak like a Cuckoo, scold like a Blue Jay, whistle like an Oriole and chuck like a Red-winged Blackbird. And it plays hide-and-seek with anyone who tries to locate it in a jungle of thickly clustered low trees and high bushes.

Look for the Chat in wet meadows that are running wild, with bushes and saplings cluttering it up and blackberry vines catching the foot to make it harder going for any invader of the Chat's domain. It is a Summer resident of the eastern United States and the Ontario section of Canada and it will advertise its appearance when it has settled in any locality for the season. It is not a bird of the woods nor a bird of cultivated land, but lives in between, favoring fields that once were cleared and cultivated but have escaped from bondage to the plow, harrow, mowing machine, and bush-hook to sprout gray birches, junipers, viburnums, dogwoods, black alders, gray alders, dogwoods, sumachs, bayberry bushes and assorted saplings all over the place. Where there is a leafy tangle of young trees, vines, and bushes on low ground or a well-watered hillside, there you will find the Chat—and hear it too. Sometimes it will give a vocal performance from a perch in the open and every so often in its enthusiasm it will let go with a bubbling roulade of melody in flight over its nest in the breeding season.

YELLOW-HEADED BLACKBIRD
(About 10 inches)

To see the Yellow-headed Blackbird is to know it and to name it is to describe it. But you have to live where it is a Summer resident or along its migration route to see it. It is distinctly a bird of the western part of North America, from the Great Plains to the Pacific Coast. Of course, birds have wings and can wander widely, but a Yellow-headed Blackbird is an uncommon sight east of the Mississippi River. In addition to the bright yellow head and vest that gives the bird its name, it has a white patch on its wing that is another clear mark of identification when it flies. The female is slightly smaller and duller, has no white wing patch, but does have a distinctly yellowish throat above its streaked under-parts. It has about the same haunts and habits as the better known and more widely distributed Red-winged Blackbird and frequently they nest together in the same marshes in the West, but in such cases the two species usually occupy different portions of the swamp. The Yellow-headed Blackbird tries hard to sing but usually gets out nothing but squeals, grunts, and a sound something like that of escaping gas. Some of the migrating flocks pillage grain fields but the birds also eat many injurious insects to strike a respectable balance.

WESTERN TANAGER
(About 6¾ inches)

The Western Tanager is a bird that wanders widely in North America and might turn up almost anywhere in Summer but the male, at least, easily would be known wherever it appeared. It is a bird with a yellow body, black wings and tail—and a red face! You might even think of it as an extra large Goldfinch with a red face. The female is a light olive-green, with slightly darker wings, and looks much like the female Scarlet Tanager except that the female Western Tanager has two distinct wing bars. The male has two wing bars also, the forward one yellow and the hind one white. The male bird loses most (or all) of its red on the face in Winter but the two wing bars distinguish the Western Tanagers from other Tanagers in any plumage. Its song is a buzzing warble something like that of the Scarlet Tanager but rougher, and its call note of "pit-ick" or "pit-er-ick" is much different from the "chip-churr!" of the Scarlet Tanager. The Western Tanager is a woodland bird for the most part, and a regular Summer resident of a broad belt running from southeastern Alaska to Texas through the western part of the United States. It does venture east of the Mississippi, however, and has straggled eastward as far as New England, which means that it's quite possible to come upon this handsome bird anywhere in the United States.

BULLOCK'S ORIOLE
(About 8¼ inches)

There are a few odd species of Oriole that may be found in the far Southwest but the two common Orioles that are Summer residents of most of North America to the fringe of the Arctic wastelands are the Baltimore Oriole and Bullock's Oriole that practically divide the continent between them, the Baltimore Oriole taking the eastern half and Bullock's Oriole the western portion. However, the Baltimore Oriole is inclinded to infringe on its cousin's territory and the ranges overlap on the Great Plains, where both species may be found regularly in the breeding season. The general color scheme of the brilliant males is the same in both species, a glowing orange body with much black on the head, wings and tail, and some white barring on the black wings. But there is little difficulty even where the species overlap in knowing the Bullock's Oriole male from the Baltimore Oriole male. The dull female and young are admittedly difficult to distinguish one from the other but the gaudy male Baltimore Oriole's head is all black, whereas the Bullock's Oriole has the bright orange of its body color on its side-face, too. Note that, from a side view, Bullock's Oriole has a black crown, an orange side-face with a black line running across it from the bill back through the eye, and a black throat. The Baltimore Oriole has a white bar on its black wing but Bullock's Oriole has a great white patch in its wing that is another distinguishing mark of the species.

In general, however, it's Bullock's Oriole that is found from the Great Plains to the Pacific Coast and it occupies the same places in that landscape and in the hearts of the inhabitants as the Baltimore Oriole does throughout the East. It is a Summer resident of the river valleys, the farmlands, the village shade trees and the woodlands, breeding as high as 6,500 feet above sea level on some of the mountainsides. It hangs its nest like the Baltimore Oriole from the outer branchlets of a shade tree, usually high above the ground and well concealed in thick foliage.

Anywhere east of the Rocky Mountains you might find a bird that looks something like the Baltimore Oriole or Bullock's Oriole but is smaller and darker than either. That would be an Orchard Oriole male, which is marked much like the male Baltimore Oriole except that it has brick red plumage where the Baltimore Oriole displays glowing orange. However, the Orchard Oriole is not nearly as abundant as the Baltimore Oriole and Bullock's Oriole, especially in the northern parts of their range, so it will be something of a prize if you see one.

[45]

INDIGO BUNTING

(About 5½ inches)

Although small, the Indigo Bunting is a conspicuous bird that sings a loud song persistently from a prominent perch, so it should be an easy bird to find if there is one in your neighborhood in June. It is a common Summer resident of central and eastern North America as far north as the Canadian border region. It's the male that you will see and hear. The female and young are dull olive-brownish birds, faintly mottled, that are always skulking along hedgerows or hiding in bushes. However, they have the same sharp call note as the male—a cross between a brief buzz and a metallic chip—and once the male is known, the female and young are soon known by association. The Indigo Bunting is a bird of the orchard, the bush country and the roadsides. It feeds regularly in thickets but the male chooses a telephone wire or the top of a fence post or small tree from which to pour forth a loud song that sounds like "sweet-sweet-sweeter-sweeter" running downhill. If the light is bad or you are not in a good position to see it, the singer may look like a black Sparrow, but a touch of sunlight on its plumage will bring out the deep blue or shining indigo that gives the bird its name.

PINE SISKIN

(About 5 inches)

The Pine Siskin looks like a small dull-colored Goldfinch with many dark stripes running over it from bill to tail, above and below. It breeds from the Canadian Border region northward and is a cold weather visitor to the United States, coming in flocks and often drifting about the country in company with the Goldfinches that it so much resembles in size, shape, flight, and general habits. Even its voice is like that of the Goldfinch except that the Siskin's voice has a wheeze or huskiness that is easy to detect and by which the bird may be known from the Goldfinch in flight overhead. The Siskin feeds mostly on seeds and may be found extracting them from pine cones, tulip tree pods, or ragweed husks. Often a walker in Winter will come upon a Black Birch that seems alive with Goldfinches and Pine Siskins pillaging the "birch cones" of the seed and, in the process, scattering a shower of dusky particles on the snow-covered ground beneath the tree. Or perhaps the Goldfinches and Siskins will be picking away on the ground at the seeds of the Sweet Gum that the winds have shaken from the pods still clinging to the bare branches above. Always look at a flock of Goldfinches in Winter. They may turn out to be Pine Siskins. Or there may be Siskins in with the Goldfinches, as is frequently the case.

ROSE-BREASTED GROSBEAK

(About 8 inches)

The male Rose-breasted Grosbeak can be offered as a model bird in every way. It is beautiful, melodious, easy to identify, beneficial to agriculture, and good to its family. It is a common Summer resident over eastern North America, more or less abundant in our woodlands, groves, orchards, and even the shade trees of suburban lawns, yet it is always a thrill to come upon this striking black and white bird with the short, thick, whitish bill and the lovely rose-colored triangle—like a bleeding heart—on its white breast. The female and young are streaked brownish birds but they are fairly easy to identify by their "gross beaks," their broad white wing bars, their white eye-lines and chin-stripes and the general shape and look of a Grosbeak about them. Furthermore, the male Grosbeak is a very affectionate mate and fond parent and if you watch the male it will not be long before he will lead you to the female or young or both. The male helps build the crude nest and takes turns with the female in sitting on the eggs. He also brings food to the female when she is on the nest and he is a good provider when the fledglings are yammering for food.

The Rose-breasted Grosbeak has a lovely song, a warbling carol with a slight baritone touch to it. The song is somewhat like the rolling carol of the Robin but sweeter and richer. Once you know the song, you will find more Rose-breasted Grosbeaks in your neighborhood than you ever suspected. They are birds that usually feed fairly high in trees and, as you walk through the fields or woods, you may hear Rose-breasted Grosbeaks singing when it is impossible to see them because of the foliage. Happily the male Rose-breasted Grosbeak often chooses a dead branch or the top branchlet of a tree as a perch from which to sing for minutes at a time, and thus you have a chance to catch up with it and see as well as hear the delightful singer.

Another obliging feature about Rose-breasted Grosbeaks is that male and female—and young, too, later in the season—frequently utter a call note that is absolutely distinctive among our native birds and an easy guide to locating any Rose-breasted Grosbeaks that may be in the vicinity. It's hard to describe bird songs or call notes so that another person will recognize them as you do, but even a hint is often a great help. In the case of the Rose-breasted Grosbeak some listeners hear this call note as a sharp "ick," while others hear it as "hic!" uttered like the first part of a hiccup. Either way, let us hope you hear it and find the bird before the male exchanges his brilliant courting costume for the streaked travel suit of Autumn and goes off with the streaked female and young to spend the Winter in Central and South America.

ROAD-RUNNER
(From 20 to 24 inches)

There seems to be general agreement that the Road-runner is quite a character. Certainly the residents and tourists of the Southwest consider it such. There is no other bird quite like it in all of North America. Here's a streaked bird that is nearly two feet long, with an odd glint in its straw-colored eye, a crest that looks like hair standing on end from fright, a long neck, a short body, powerful legs, and an absurdly long tail that the owner often raises and lowers slowly like the boom of a derrick. Of course, there is never any difficulty about identifying a Road-runner. The difficulty is to see it. You have to live in—or visit—the cactus and mesquite country of the Southwest to see and hear this strange bird. The sounds that it makes are as strange as its appearance and habits. It may purr like a cat, coo like a Dove, "cuck" like a Cuckoo, squawk like a Jay or make a loud rattling sound by "clacking" its bill rapidly.

The Road-runner is found all through the arid regions of the Southwest but it is not easily found at all times. If you go out looking for a Road-runner, either because you want to see one yourself or you wish to point out this odd bird to some distinguished visitor, you will discover that the sometimes bold and even impudent Road-runner can be a very shy and evasive bird at other moments.

These picturesque birds pick a living from the ground, eating grasshoppers in large quantities and gobbling down such other desert tidbits as centipedes, lizards, mice and small snakes, including some poisonous species. They build large nests of twigs about a foot or two above the ground in some cactus cluster or scrub growth of bush or tree, and the female lays 4 to 6 eggs in a clutch. It's a comparatively rare thing to see a Road-runner on the wing, though the birds can fly well enough and occasionally do. But they much prefer running to flying and they have been timed ahead of automobiles running as fast as 18 miles an hour. When chased by man, beast, or car, they lean over like sprinters, hold their long tails level behind them and bound away on apparently tireless legs. When a bird is ready to stop, it throws up its long tail and uses it as an "air brake."

Though it has been proved by examination of their stomachs that Road-runners are beneficial birds, they may take a few Quail eggs from time to time. This has led some thoughtless hunters to demand that Road-runners be shot on sight. On the other hand, most inhabitants of the area where these birds are resident look upon the Road-runner as a vastly amusing and picturesque bird and a notable addition to the wildlife of the Southwest.

PURPLE FINCH
(About 6 inches)

Purple Finches are abundant and delightful little birds that are resident over much of the continent of North America and may be encountered anywhere at any time in this country and Canada, but they are not always easy to recognize at first glance for several reasons. One reason is that most of the Purple Finches you may come upon will have little or no purple on them, and another is that there are other birds with which they might easily be confused. Only the male Purple Finch in good plumage has much purple about it and then it's more of a raspberry or "old rose" color that looks as though it had been poured over the birds head and allowed to trickle down over the body and wings. The female and young are gray-brown birds with dark streaks. They are chunkier than Sparrows, have thicker bills and may be recognized by their heavier heads and a rather heavy grayish line on the side-face running backward from the eye.

There will be no problem at all as soon as you learn the song of the Purple Finch, a delightful rolling warble that differs much from the songs of any other birds with which it might be confused by sight except the House Finch of the West. The Purple Finch also has a call note that is even more decisive, because no other native bird—not even the House Finch—makes a sound like it. The call note sounds like a metallic "tick" or "click," thin but clear. Once that is learned, the Purple Finch will be no problem.

HOUSE FINCH
(About 5½ inches)

The House Finch of the West—most abundant in the Southwest—is much like the Purple Finch in appearance and also in its warbled song. However, there are little differences that are easily noted where the ranges of these birds overlap because the House Finch is well named, likes to nest in vines on porches, and is easily inspected at close range. It doesn't take long to note that the House Finch is a smaller and more finely streaked bird than the Purple Finch. The color on the male Purple Finch usually is deepest on the head, whereas the color on the male House Finch is deepest on the throat and upper breast. Also the color on the male House Finch is a brighter red than the "old rose" of the Purple Finch. The rather broad grayish line on the side of the head of the female or young Purple Finch will help to distinguish it from the female or young House Finch. Another point is that the Purple Finch does not have such a fondness for dooryards, telephone wires and human companionship. The House Finch of the West is like the English Sparrow in its desire to make itself at home where people live, but the native bird has much better manners and a much finer song than the interloper from Europe.

YELLOW-BILLED CUCKOO

(About 12½ inches)

We have two species of Cuckoo that are Summer residents the length and breadth of the land. They are the Black-billed Cuckoo and the Yellow-billed Cuckoo. They are the same size and color and have the same haunts and habits, yet it is not difficult to know one from the other if you can get a clear view of the birds because the Yellow-billed Cuckoo has some "positive identification marks" about it. Both Cuckoos are long slim birds with slightly curved bills and long tails. They are a soft olive-brown above and clear white underneath except that their tail feathers are dark on the underside, with some white spotting. One point of difference between the species is that the tail of the Yellow-billed Cuckoo is darker on the underside and has large round white spots in it. The underside of the tail of the Black-billed Cuckoo is more grayish and the white spots are more like ovals or half-moons than circles. If the bird is in a tree overhead, this difference may be noted. If you see the bird's bill you will know the species because the lower half of the Yellow-billed Cuckoo's bill is yellow, except for the black tip. In many cases it is a bright yellow that edges over to the upper bill near the base and it can be noted at a fair distance. If the Cuckoo is in flight, the Yellow-billed Cuckoo will show a bright cinnamon patch in its wing. Our Cuckoos are beneficial birds that build their own nests and eat many harmful caterpillars.

CEDAR WAXWING

(About 7½ inches)

The Cedar Waxwing must be the most polite bird in the world. Sometimes in June or July there will be rows of Cedar Waxwings sitting on a branch of a cherry tree passing a cherry from bill to bill up and down the line, each bird apparently too polite to swallow the cherry and put an end to the performance. It's easy to know them because of their abundance and their neat little crests, and it's easy to fall in love with them because of their soft coloring, their gentle ways and friendly dispositions. The chocolate-brown plumage is soft and silky, with traces of pink and mauve in it here and there. There is some gray in its wings and darker gray in the tail with a bright yellow band at the end. The bird has a black chin and a brief black line running up from the base of the bill through the eye to the edge of the crest. Cedar Waxwings are found all over North America but in cold weather most of the birds of the northern area drift southward for comfort. They are sometimes called Cedar Birds or Cherry Birds but the reason for the name "Waxwing" is that at the ends of some of the wing feathers (called secondaries) there are tips of a substance that looks exactly like bright red sealing wax. The one thing these lovely birds lack is a fine song. All they can offer is a slurred series of soft notes that sound like "a string of beads."

GREAT HORNED OWL
(From 18 to 23 inches)

Owls are birds that are more often heard than seen. There are many species in North America, one of the largest and most powerful species being the Great Horned Owl. Among the Owls and the birds of prey in general the females usually are larger than the males; a female Great Horned Owl may be nearly two feet in length, with talons like hooks of steel. The "horns," of course, are merely ear-tufts that serve as definite identification marks for the Great Horned Owl. No other North American Owl of that size has such conspicuous ear-tufts. The Long-eared Owl is far smaller and its "long ears" are much closer together on top of its head.

The Great Horned Owl is one of the fiercest hunters of the wildwood. It will attack birds as large as Canada Geese and it catches Grouse, Pheasant, and Quail, as well as many other birds. Perhaps the easiest way to find a Great Horned Owl is to go to any spot where Crows are circling and swooping wildly around an evergreen tree, cawing loudly all the time. They heckle and badger the larger Hawks in that manner, too. The Hawks usually are more in the open, either on a conspicuous perch or soaring in circles with the flock of cawing Crows in cautious pursuit. But if the excited Crows are swooping at something in an evergreen, it's probably an Owl of some kind that is the object of their noisy

attention and it may be that terror of the woods, the Great Horned Owl, sitting on a branch close to the trunk of the tree staring disdainfully at the swooping and circling mob of Crows.

It's a mistake to think that Owls are blind in the daytime. They see very well in broad daylight, but their eyes are better adapted than the eyes of other birds and most animals for seeing in dim light, and that's why they hunt in the dusk and the dark of night. Under such conditions they have a decided advantage over their prey. Other things that favor them when hunting in the dark is that they have remarkably keen hearing and their flight is practically noiseless. They often drop on their hapless victims unseen and unheard. They pursue all kinds of small mammals and apparently smell is a trifling thing in the lives of Great Horned Owls because they seem to relish skunks as much as they do rabbits. Owls swallow bones, pelts, and all, and the bones, fur, teeth, and claws of mice, rats, and other such prey are later ejected from the Owl's mouth in the form of pellets. A searcher for Owls often will go through the woods with his eyes on the ground, looking for Owl pellets under trees that might harbor such birds. The pellets of the Great Horned Owl are three or four inches long and an inch thick.

These large, fierce and hardy birds often begin nesting in late February or early March when snow is still on the ground and in the air.

SCREECH OWL

(About 10 inches)

This is the bird with the ghostly tremulous wailing cry that Henry David Thoreau, hearing in his nights at Walden Pond, described as the voice of a lost soul crying: "O-o-o-o that I had never been bor-r-r-rn." It runs along on one pitch for a few notes and then descends in a quavering scale to fade out in the silence and gloom of the night. It is one of the small members of the Owl family—about the size of a Robin—and is a common permanent resident throughout North America. The really odd thing about the Screech Owl is that it comes in two colors—red and gray. There are many birds that change color from Summer to Winter and there are many species in which the males are one color and the females another color. But Screech Owls do not change the color of their plumage from one season to another, nor does the male wear one color and the female another. The simple fact is that some Screech Owls are reddish-brown with lighter and darker dots and streaks that give them a mottled appearance and other Screech Owls are grayish-brown with the same assortment of dots and streaks to give the mottled appearance. But whether it is a Screech Owl of the "rufous phase" or the "gray phase," as the scientists put it, it will be known from other small Owls by its distinct ear-tufts. Sight unseen, of course, it may be known by its mournful, quavering, descending, wailing cry.

Screech Owls live in woodlands and groves and orchards and the shade trees of village streets and suburban lawns. Usually they nest in holes in trees but they will also occupy cavities in barns or other buildings and they will accept bird boxes with suitable openings if they consider the locations favorable. Furthermore, they will often use these same boxes, cavities, or holes in trees as dwelling places or retreats from enemies and bad weather at any time of year. Screech Owls have been seen sunning themselves on bright Winter days in the doorways of their retreats, and it's curious to note that most of the holes in trees that the Screech Owls choose for themselves have a "southern exposure," presumably for that purpose as well as to escape some of the Winter snow that so often is carried along by a wind whipping down from the North.

Because they do most of their hunting in the dusk or at night, Screech Owls often are unsuspected neighbors around our homes. But if they venture out in broad daylight we will hear about it from other birds that will gather around to shriek at any member of the Owl family. Occasionally a Blue Jay, inspecting a hole in a tree as a source of supply of acorns stored away by a squirrel, will find a Screech Owl tenant at home and sound an alarm to wake the neighborhood. We should be glad to have Screech Owls as neighbors because they are beneficial birds whose chief items of diet are insects and mice.

NIGHTHAWK
(About 9½ inches)

The Nighthawk is no Hawk at all but an insect-eating bird that is a first cousin of the Whip-poor-will that it much resembles in appearance and general habits. In flight both species look like great dark Swallows but there is an easy way of knowing one bird from the other. The Nighthawk has a conspicuous white patch toward the outer end of each wing that shows clearly in flight. If there are Nighthawks around—and they are Summer residents of most of North America—you will not only see them but hear them in the dusk, which is their time for hunting insects on the wing. Whether it be over crowded cities, little villages, or lonely stretches of open country, of a Summer eve these wonderful acrobats of the air wheel, whirl, dive down and zoom upward through the twilight and dusk, catching insects at every turn and uttering a loud, buzzing, nasal "be-e-eent!" all the while. They make no nests. In the country they lay their 2 eggs on the bare ground and in cities they deposit their eggs on flat graveled roofs. In the Autumn the Nighthawks gather in great flocks for the southward migration, heading down the broad river valleys, whirling about the skies with their white wing patches for positive identification marks but looking more than ever like gigantic and magnificent Swallows.

WHIP-POOR-WILL
(About 10 inches)

It seems almost a waste of words to describe a Whip-poor-will because so few persons ever see it compared to the many who know it by the weird vibrant call that gives the bird its name. It is, however, much like the Nighthawk in appearance and habits, a chunky, dark, wide-mouthed, insect-eating bird with a short curved bill, a white band across its lower throat, and white patches on the outer feathers of its tail. Unlike the Nighthawk that whirls through the upper air for its prey, the Whip-poor-will stays close to the ground in river valleys or watered meadows and gathers insects in short low flights. It drifts like a shadow through the gloom, rarely rising to a height so that its form can be seen against the sky. It may give its throbbing call from the bare ground, from a smooth stone, or from a lengthwise position on a fence rail or limb of a tree, with a preliminary "chuck" and a deep nod at each "WILL" of its repeated call: "Whip-poor-WILL! Whip-poor-WILL! Whip-poor-WILL!" Sometimes of warm moonlit night it will call and fly about to feed from dusk till dawn. It lays its 2 eggs in a depression on the ground in the woods or on a brushy hillside. It drifts southward almost unnoticed on migration, an unseen bird that is known to many only as a throbbing call in the hush of Summer eves.

DOWNY WOODPECKER
(About 6½ inches)

This is probably the most common, friendly, and widespread representative of the Woodpecker family in all of North America. It may be found in our woods, on our farms, in our parks, and around our homes Winter and Summer. It is one of the midget members of its great family and a plain black and white bird except in one respect; the male wears a red patch on the back of its head. There is another member of the family that looks almost exactly like the Downy Woodpecker but in a larger size. That's the Hairy Woodpecker, which is also found the length and breadth of the country but is not so abundant or so friendly a bird as the little Downy.

If the two birds are seen together, the Hairy will look almost twice as large as the Downy, though the real difference is not nearly that much. But when the birds are seen alone, it is sometimes difficult to estimate the exact size. In such a case, look at the bill of the bird. The Hairy Woodpecker has a much heavier and longer bill in comparison with the size of the bird itself. After a few trials, this difference will be clear to the eye. There is a difference in the notes, too. The call note of the Hairy is much firmer and louder and the clattering cry of the bigger bird is sustained in pitch, whereas the notes of the Downy are descending at the finish. The little Downy is much the friendlier and will be a daily dooryard visitor in Winter if a supply of suet is offered as a lure.

YELLOW-BILLED SAPSUCKER
(About 8½ inches)

Despite its name, this is a Woodpecker and looks and acts much like other members of the family except that, over much of its range in eastern North America, it is a Summer resident or migrant where other Woodpeckers are sedate and respectable permanent residents. If you see a Woodpecker between the size of the Downy and the Hairy Woodpecker with a red forehead, a black band across its breast, yellowish on its speckled under parts and a vertical white patch in its wing, that will be the Yellow-bellied Sapsucker. There are other kinds of Sapsuckers in the western part of the country that differ in plumage but all the males can be identified by the yellow on the under parts and the vertical white patch in the wing. The Yellow-bellied Sapsucker is the only smallish Woodpecker over its range with a red forehead patch. The male also has a red throat where the female wears white. The bird gets its name from its habit of drinking the sap that oozes from the regular rows of holes that it drills in the bark of trees, particularly apple trees. It also eats insects that come to drink the sap, and has a squealing, whining cry that it utters frequently.

[54]

PILEATED WOODPECKER

(About 18 inches)

Think of a Woodpecker as large as a Crow! A great black and white bird with a flaming red crest! That's the Pileated Woodpecker that is still to be found throughout the wooded regions of North America. Once upon a time the even larger Ivory-billed Woodpecker might have been seen or heard in the big timber of the river bottoms of the South, but now the Ivory-billed Woodpecker is sought in vain through its old haunts. Perhaps it is extinct. At any rate, if you see a huge Woodpecker with a red crest, a flashing and magnificent bird, it will be the Pileated Woodpecker that happily still seems to be holding its own in the forests of the United States and Canada. You can't fail to identify it immediately if you have the luck to see one. It is our only Woodpecker of that size and the only Woodpecker of North America that has a crest.

The Pileated Woodpecker has a repeated cry much like that of the "wicker" of the Flicker, but the voice of the Pileated is more "throaty." It's difficult to describe the difference but where both birds are resident it soon is easy to distinguish one call from the other. When a Pileated goes to work on a tree to dig out grubs or adult bettles with its great bill, it certainly makes the chips fly. It whacks away with terrific force and from a distance it often sounds as though a man were chopping in the woods. An odd point is that sometimes a woodchopper at work will find that the blows of his axe have "called" a Pileated Woodpecker to the vicinity.

Though they are distinctly woodland birds, these big Woodpeckers swing out into the open when going from one place to another to feed. Sometimes they have favorite dead trees to which they resort regularly with no intention of hammering or hacking away at the glistening bare trunk or the ghostly gray branches. They merely loaf about the tree, edging slowly upward or backing slowly downward as they utter their loud calls at intervals. Where a ridge has been lumbered they will come frequently to inspect the old stumpage in search of grubs or grown beetles. If they find a stump that is a storehouse of these dainties, they will return at odd moments until they have picked it clean. In addition to their normal insect diet, they will eat some berries in season and they seem to have a real fondness for wild grapes in Autumn.

Almost any hole in any tree may be the work of a member of the Woodpecker family but where the Pileated has been at work the traces are unmistakable. This bird hews out rectangular hollows that look like topless boxes and it rips off heavy strips of bark that no other member of the family could begin to remove.

RUBY-THROATED HUMMINGBIRD
(About 3½ inches)

The simple facts about Hummingbirds are like the birds themselves, almost unbelievable. These are the smallest birds in the whole world. There are some 500 species and only one species is over 5 inches in length, long bill included. They are real all-America birds, found only from Patagonia to the Canadian woods, but most of the 500 species are tropical and only a dozen or so species are more or less common Summer residents of different sections of the United States. Only a single species is found regularly east of the Mississippi. That's the Ruby-throated Hummingbird that derives its name from the glittering gorget worn by the male and displayed at its brightest about the time that the female is building its marvelous little nest neatly balanced on an apple twig in an old orchard.

The Ruby-throated Hummingbird is "about as big as a minute" and weighs about as much as a copper cent. Like all Hummingbirds it has a tiny body, a long, thin, tube-like bill, iridescent plumage, and a wing motion so rapid that it is almost invisible to the eye. All we see is a blur where the wings are beating in the air as the bird hovers in front of some flower or flits about the garden with the humming sound that gives the bird its name. The hum comes from the rapid vibration of the wings. The voice of the Hummingbird is a sharp squeak or tiny buzz and usually is heard when males are quarreling over mates or territorial rights in the breeding season.

There are certain things that Hummingbirds like and certain conditions that please them. If these things are provided, Hummingbirds will visit you. They like water, though not necessarily in large quantities. But they like well watered meadows, especially where the brooks are lined with wild flowers. On the West Coast some of the abundant species will settle for bird baths and lawn sprinklers as all the water they need and will build their dainty downy nests in porch vines, but the Ruby-throated Hummingbird of the East is not quite that much domesticated. It will feed among the dooryard flowers and porch vines, but its tiny nest is hidden away on the limb of some shade tree or fruit tree around the yard, out in the orchard or down the road. A half-dollar would cover nest, eggs and all. There are 2 tiny eggs to a clutch and there may be one or two broods a year.

Hummingbirds are courageous little birds, often fighting among themselves or with other birds around the dooryard. They dart about with such speed that, with their needle-like bills, they look quite dangerous, but it's a rare thing for them to come to actual blows. They are such marvelous creatures on the wing that they can not only fly backward as well as forward but they can swing in the air from side to side as though they were riding on a pendulum.

PURPLE MARTIN
(About 8 inches)

This is the largest and darkest of our Swallows and it may be found as a Summer resident almost anywhere in North America. The male is a steely blue-black and, unlike our other Swallows, is practically the same color below as above. The female is duller above and grayish below. Because they are insect-eaters and sweep tirelessly through the air all day in pursuit of mosquitoes and other insect pests, Purple Martins have been cherished birds in this country since Indian days. The Indians used to hang out lines of dried gourds as nesting places for the birds in their villages. Early white settlers followed the custom and their descendants went on to make architectural improvements in the Martin dwellings. The Martins take naturally to community life and some of the elaborate structures now offered them as Summer homes look exactly like huge apartment houses for birds. English Sparrows and Starlings, by taking their nesting sites, have driven the Martins away from some sections of the country in which they were formerly abundant, notably New England, but efforts are being made to lure these feathered favorites back to their old homes again.

TREE SWALLOW
(About 6 inches)

The flashing Tree Swallow that sweeps in chattering flight over our Summer meadows is just as widespread over North America as its larger cousin, the Purple Martin. With bright sunlight on its plumage, the Tree Swallow is a metallic greenish-black above and clear white underneath. This contrast in color above and below makes it easy to distinguish from all our other native Swallows except the Violet-green Swallow of the West. But the Violet-green Swallow has two white patches that show clearly on its rump, whereas the Tree Swallow is a solid dark color above. In the wild state the Tree Swallow nests in holes in trees or crevices in rocks, but again like the Purple Martin, the bird has become half-domesticated to the extent that it will not only accept bird boxes put out as nesting places but will go looking for them and return year after year to nest in the same boxes. The Tree Swallow is the hardiest of the family and is usually the first to arrive in Spring and the last to leave in the Autumn. It gathers in great flocks for the Autumn migration to the Gulf Coast area where the birds spend the Winter.

LOGGERHEAD SHRIKE

(About 9 inches)

Shrikes are striking birds in color and habits. For their striking habits they are often called "Butcher Birds." If you see a dead grasshopper, mouse, or small bird hanging on a thorn in a bush or stuck on a barbed wire fence, that will be the work of the "Butcher Bird" or Shrike. There are two resident species in North America. The Northern Shrike is the larger and the more northerly in range. The Loggerhead Shrike is much more common and widespread over the United States, particularly in the southern half of the country. Otherwise the two Shrikes look much alike and act in the same murderous manner. They are generally grayish above and white below, with a heavy black line running back from the thickish black bill through the eye. They have black wings with white patches, and black tails fringed with white that shows best in flight. The Loggerhead Shrike is somewhat like the Mockingbird in color but not at all like it in voice or actions. The best the Loggerhead can do in song is a few gurgle-like notes and a buzz. The Mockingbird lacks the heavy black line through the eye that the Shrike wears.

HORNED LARK

(About 7½ inches)

This is a soft-colored, mild-mannered little bird of the open country, of wide plains, of barren territory almost bare of herbage, of the dunes by the seashore, of pasture land that has been closely cropped by cattle, of flat areas like the airports that now dot the country, and of those well-groomed gems of greenery, the golf courses of the United States and Canada. There probably is no golf course in North America that doesn't have, in the course of a year, more Horned Larks than members walking the fairways. These birds are a tan-brown above and grayish below. They have black on their foreheads, a black patch that starts back from the bill and drops below the eye, and a black band across the upper breast. There may be much or little yellow between the black patches on the bird's head and breast. The plumage varies in different parts of North America and at different seasons of the year. You have to move slowly and look carefully to find Horned Larks feeding because their color blends with the grass or ground. The birds crouch low when feeding and sometimes creep almost like mice through the short grass or over the bare ground. Do not look for the "horns" of the Horned Lark. They are usually invisible, if not imaginary.

HERRING GULL

(From 23 to 26 inches)

The Gulls of our lakes, rivers, harbors, and ocean shores are large birds—gigantic compared with our Sparrows and Warblers—and wonderful fliers. They are also noisy and numerous and there are so many different species that look much alike that it is a problem for the beginner to tell them apart. The best way to make a start is to get to know one Gull with certainty and use that as a standard. The Herring Gull is the best standard because it is the most abundant Gull of North America. It sits about on piers, buoys, rocks, beaches, and sand bars and is readily available for close inspection, which makes it an easy bird to know.

The first impression on looking at a group of Gulls, whether at rest or on the wing, is that there are "white ones" and "brown ones." The "white ones" are seldom completely white and the "brown ones" are really speckled or mottled, but the important distinction is that the "white ones" are the adult birds and the mottled ones are the younger ones. The young of all species of Gull are mottled and it takes them from two to four years—depending upon the species—to come of age in adult plumage and be one of the "white ones" in a Gull group. If the "white ones" are loked over carefully, it is seen that most of them have some gray or blue or black in their plumage. If the darker color is on the upper surface of the wings and across the back, it is known as a "mantle."

The adult Herring Gull may be known by its size, its blue-gray mantle with blackish wing tips and its *pale flesh-colored legs.* The color of the legs is most important because it sets the Herring Gull apart from such others as the Ring-billed Gull and the California Gull that, though smaller, are much like the Herring Gull in plumage. Once the adult Herring Gull is definitely identified, it is fairly simple to move ahead and identify other common species by the items in which they differ from the Herring Gull.

COMMON TERN

(From 13 to 16 inches)

Terns in flight over the ocean are certainly among the most beautiful and graceful birds in the world. They are often called Sea Swallows and it is a good name for them. They look like large black-capped white Swallows as they wheel and whirl in their ceaseless offshore patrol along our coast lines. They are, on the average, much smaller and thinner than Gulls and, as further marks of distinction ,the Terns have more or less deeply forked tails and sharp pointed bills. Even at a distance Terns can be known from Gulls by their lighter and more dashing flight and by their habit of plunging head-first into the ocean in pursuit of the small fish or other aquatic creatures on which they feed.

But Terns are like Gulls in one discouraging way: there are many different species and some of them look so much alike that only the field experts can tell them apart on the wing. Where there are four species that so closely resemble one another in size and plumage as the Common Tern, Roseate Tern, Forster's Tern and Arctic Tern, the expert tells them apart by their voices, a bit of light or dark shading on the back or the underside of the wings, the depth of the fork in the tail and the differences in the color of the bill.

The Common Tern and Forster's Tern are so much alike in general appearance, even to the orange-red color of the bill, that the beginner might give up hope of ever knowing one bird from the other, but there are small differences that are not too difficult to note if the birds are seen regularly at close range. From a top view the primaries (large outer flight feathers of the wing) of the Common Tern are dark compared to the remainder of the wing and in the Forster's Tern the primaries are lighter than the remainder of the wing. Also, the upper surface of the tail of the Common Tern is white whereas it is gray for the Forster's Tern. Still, it does take time and patience to learn these things.

COMMON LOON
(From 28 to 36 inches)

If Loons had lawyers they could sue persons who use the phrase "as crazy as a Loon." They are not crazy birds by any means. On the contrary, Loons are wise birds and it is difficult to get near them. The slanderous reference to their alleged lack of sanity grew out of the weird calls they utter on their breeding grounds and Summer haunts—repeated shrieks and chattering hoots that sound like hollow mockery or demoniac laughter echoing over a lonely lake or a melancholy marsh. Loons are among the most "watery" of our water birds and, indeed, are rarely seen out of water. Their feet are not placed or formed so they can walk comfortably on dry ground. The best they can do is an awkward waddle. In the water, however, they are altogether at home. Loons are large, dark-colored, sharp-billed diving birds that look like Geese at a distance on the water, but they may be known from Geese by their "flat heads," their sharp bills, and their habit of "sitting" much lower in the water.

The Common Loon in Summer plumage has a shining greenish-black head and neck, a white breast, and a general "body color" that from a distance looks all dark but on closer inspection is a delightful checkered pattern of little white squares and dots on a black background. On the side of the dark neck there is a horizontal white patch with vertical black lines running through it, but you have to be real close to see these lovely markings.

Loons are, for the most part, fresh-water birds through the Spring and Summer. They breed in the reeds around ponds and lakes, many of them in uninhabited areas, feeding themselves and their young on fish, shrimp, frogs, and even an occasional vegetable salad of marsh plants. In the Autumn migration they appear in great numbers along our coasts and they dive so deep for fish that they have been caught in nets 90 feet below the surface. They used their half-closed wings as well as their feet in swimming under water, and those who have seen it say that the birds seem to be actually flying through the water in pursuit of their prey.

SPOTTED SANDPIPER
(About 7½ inches)

Sandpipers are small birds with long thin bills and little legs and feet that seem to twinkle as they run rapidly along our ocean beaches, mud flats and lake shores in search of food at the fringe of the water. There are many kinds of Sandpiper but probably the best known and the most widespread of the family in North America is the Spotted Sandpiper, which may be found anywhere in the United States or Canada in the warmer months

of the year. Whether it is an ocean beach or just the drinking hole for cattle on a farm, the Spotted Sandpiper will be there. It is greenish-brown above and white beneath, with a distinct white line through the eye and its white breast plentifully sprinkled with dark spots. It also shows a white line in the wing when flying and when it is standing still it has a curious "teetering" motion of the body. It seems to be trying a balancing act by lowering its head and raising the tail and rear part of the body. The young of the year have no spots and the parent birds lose the spots before going southward in the Autumn.

SOLITARY SANDPIPER
(About 8½ inches)

The Spotted Sandpiper is found on ocean beaches as well as around farm ponds, but the Solitary Sandpiper is a rare sight on an ocean beach. It takes to the inland swamps, the country ponds, and the lakes in the woods. It even nests in bushes or trees, like a Robin. In fact, it will use a Robin's nest after the real owners have abandoned it. The Solitary Sandpiper is a bit larger than the Spotted Sandpiper that is found as a Summer resident over the same territory and there are other differences that are easily noticed. The Spotted Sandpiper has a solid greenish-brown coat for its upper parts whereas the Solitary Sandpiper wears a pepper-and-salt mixture, a speckled grayish coat above. The throat and sides of the breast of the Solitary Sandpiper are sprinkled lightly with fine spots where the Spotted Sandpiper in the breeding season has much heavier spots. The eye-line of the Spotted Sandpiper is distinct and in the Solitary Sandpaper it is vague. Also, the Solitary shows a dark center line in its tail with much white on either side in flight. And finally the Spotted Sandpiper "teeters" with its hind parts whereas the Solitary Sandpiper jerks and bobs its head more in its "teetering" performances.

GREAT BLUE HERON

(From 42 to 52 inches)

This is probably the tallest native bird that you will see standing on two legs. There are a few others that may run taller—the Great White Heron, the Whooping Crane, the Sandhill Crane—but these are rare or, at least, uncommon sights around the country whereas the Great Blue Heron is a common permanent resident of most of the United States and a regular Summer resident of all of North America to the edge of the Arctic tundra. Where the Great Blue Heron and the Sandhill Crane or Little Brown Crane are found in the same regions, the birds can be identified in the air at considerable heights because, though Cranes and Herons alike fly with their long legs trailing out behind, the Cranes fly with their necks stretched to full length whereas Herons fly with their necks folded back in a flat "S" loop.

Herons belong to a group of birds that the scientists call "waders" because they walk about in the water or marshy places in search of food. For that purpose they are equipped with long legs, long necks, and long sharp bills. The Great Blue Heron stands about 4 feet tall and has a long sharp bill that can be a dangerous weapon when the bird is attacked. It feeds in swamps and marshes as well as along streams, rivers, and lakes. It will eat fish, frogs, shrimps, crayfish, salamanders, aquatic insects, and practically anything else it finds in the water. It will sometimes move to higher ground and dine on mice, grasshoppers,

and beetles of various kinds. Fishermen say that it catches trout before they can get around to it themselves and for that reason they dislike the bird.

Great Blue Herons are lone hunters most of the time but in the breeding season they gather in colonies and nest together in trees or high bushes in swamp rookeries. When the young are growing up these rookeries are noisy and smelly places, filled with the grunts and squawks of old and young and the decaying remains of infertile eggs, lost food and other waste material from the nests. But once the young Herons are able to fend for themselves, the old birds part company and go on their lone hunting trips again. When ice forms on the lakes, ponds, and rivers of the northern part of the country, the Herons have to move southward to find food. Many of them move coastward at the same time and Great Blue Herons are numerous in our coastal marshes all through the colder months. Those that breed in the northern sectors will move in that direction as soon as the ice goes out in Spring.

PIED-BILLED GREBE
(From 12 to 15 inches)

Grebes are water birds that, from their size and general shape, might be mistaken for Ducks at a distance but they have pointed bills, sit much lower in the water than Ducks do and look as though they had no tails. Hunters often refer to them as "Hell-divers" because they dive so quickly and stay down so long. They have the ability to sink their bodies in the water and keep just their heads stuck up like periscopes. They do this when they are suspicious or frightened and wish to keep out of sight as much as possible. The Pied-billed Grebe is the smallest and most widespread of our common Grebes. It may be found as a Summer resident on almost any body of water, small or large, in North America. However, it does prefer the smaller ones and it breeds regularly in our inland swamps and marshes and in the reeds sorrounding our lakes and ponds. Seen on the water—and it is rarely seen out of the water—it is a small, dark, "roundish" bird with a somewhat snaky neck and head and a Chicken-like bill with a black band around it, the feature that gives the bird its name. Perhaps the only remarkable thing about the "Dabchick," as it is sometimes called, is its voice, a long loud call of "cow-cow-cow" repeated many times in the breeding season.

GREEN HERON
(From 16 to 22 inches)

In all of North America there is hardly a river, lake, marsh, swamp, pond, or water hole that isn't visited by a Green Heron at some time or other in warm weather. It is easily the best known, the most abundant and the most widespread of our Herons and has many different names given to it by farm boys. Its official name is the only confusing thing about this familiar bird. Why Green Heron? To most observers it shows more slate-blue or an even darker shade on most of its upper plumage. The crown is greenish-black and the feathers form something of a low raggedy crest at times. The neck is chestnut-reddish with a cream-colored streak running down the front and widening on the breast. When the Green Heron is flushed from its perch or from a feeding site in a bog it flaps away with a cry of "ske-ow!" if it makes any sound at all. Green Herons build crude nests in bushes or trees overhanging a pond, lake, marsh, or some other watery area. They eat the usual Heron diet and drift southward as soon as their Summer haunts are frozen over by cold weather.

[64]

BLACK-CROWNED NIGHT HERON

(From 23 to 28 inches)

The name Black-crowned Night Heron accurately describes the bird and gives a hint of its habits. It has a conspicuous blackish crown and it does a good deal of wandering about in the night when most other birds are asleep. It is a Heron that is easy to become acquainted with because of its large size, its abundance in North America and a notable but invisible feature, its voice. Henry Wadsworth Longfellow wrote in "Paul Revere's Ride" that to some of his alarmed countrymen of that era the patriotic silversmith on his immortal ride was

A voice in the darkness, a knock at the door,
And a word that shall echo forevermore!

The Black-crowned Night Heron is like Paul Revere to some extent. It doesn't go around knocking on doors but to many of our countrymen it is only a voice in the darkness, a strange sound in the night. As it flies silently through the dusk or dark from one feeding ground to another, the Night Heron now and then utters a loud "quawk!" that must startle any listener below, certainly the first time he hears it. Doubtless there are some dwellers in rural districts who know this bird only by ear and after dark; they never have seen it. It is, however, easy enough to find by daylight if there are any fair-sized marshy areas or bodies of water nearby. It is much more common near the coast than it is inland but it can be found almost anywhere in the United States where there is open water. It usually nests in trees in marshy or swampy areas, often in rookeries of considerable size.

The adult birds have greenish-black crowns and backs, blue-gray wings and white under-parts. There is a white patch on the forehead that can be seen if you are close to the bird. The bill is long, heavy, and dark and the legs of the bird are yellow. The young are grayish-brown with many light streaks and spots. There are only a few other marsh birds with which the young or adult Black-crowned Night Heron can be confused. There is a more southerly Yellow-crowned Night Heron that is about the same size but the head pattern is quite different. The young of the two Night Herons, however, are quite similar and hard to distinguish from one another in the field. There is also the American Bittern, which is a streaked bird of approximately the same pattern and size as young Night Herons, but the large Bittern is a rare sight compared to the common young Night Herons that wander about the country. The young Black-crowned Night Herons often are perched in trees. Bitterns are generally on the ground in a bog.

KILLDEER
(About 10 inches)

The Killdeer is a handsome, abundant, friendly, and most obliging bird. It stays out in the open where it can be seen and it announces itself by name quite clearly, calling "Kill-dee" at intervals in its flight. It is about the size of a Robin, a tannish-brown above, clear white below and it has two distinct black bands across its breast. It also shows a beautiful salmon-pink on its lower back and upper tail surface as it flies off. The Killdeer is a member of the Plover family and Plovers are classed as shore birds, but the Killdeer is only occasionally a bird of our ocean beaches or tidal mud flats. It is found inland all over North America through most of the year. It does play along the shores of rivers, lakes, and ponds but, on the whole, it prefers football fields, golf courses, the flat surfaces of airports, plowed ground—any place in the open where the grass is short or the ground is bare. It is an abundant bird on farm lands and likes to roam the close-cropped pastures with the cattle. When they are disturbed at night among the cattle they go flying around in the darkness uttering their plaintive cries of "Kill-dee, kill-dee, kill-dee," with an occasional purring note or skittering trill thrown in for added weird effect.

RUDDY TURNSTONE
(About 9 inches)

This shore bird on the wing looks like a flying marble cake. It displays a striking pattern of orange-red, jet black and pure white in a delightful way. There can be no chance of mistaking it for any other bird in flight but when the Ruddy Turnstone is feeding along our coasts it is often difficult to find on pebbled beaches or rocky headlands because there its mixture of colors may blend with the background. It is well named, because it turns over stones with its stout bill to get at the food it finds in such places. It looks like a small, squat, multi-colored Dove with bright orange legs and feet. Many of our shore birds are difficult to know, one from the other, because they are of a size and look so much alike, but the Ruddy Turnstone is a most satis-factory bird. There is no other shore bird anything like it except the Black Turn-stone, which is easily distinguished because it is much darker, has a completely black head and lacks the orange-red upper parts of the Ruddy Turnstone. Also, the Black Turnstone is a West Coast bird whereas the Ruddy Turnstone is found along both coasts and on the Great Lakes.

AMERICAN EGRET

(From 35 to 42 inches)

This is a large white Heron somewhat smaller than the Great Blue Heron and, as a rule, living somewhat more to the southward. However, the protection afforded these beautiful birds in the past quarter of a century has increased their numbers so much that they have been edging northward steadily so that now, especially after the breeding season, they may be found wandering as far north as the Canadian border region. Years ago the Egrets were harried almost to extinction by plume hunters for the millinery trade, who invaded their community breeding grounds and killed the parent birds on the nests for the "aigrettes" they display in the breeding season. Of course, when the parents were killed, the young birds were left to starve. This horrible practice was stopped by law and rigid enforcement and now Egrets may be seen almost anywhere in the United States either as Summer visitors, Summer residents or—in the warmer sections—permanent residents.

Since the Great White Heron is confined to the Florida Keys, there are only three large white birds of the Heron type that may be found over most of the United States. They are the American Egret, the Snowy Egret, and the immature Little Blue Heron that starts out with all-white plumage and doesn't reach the full blue stage until it is 3 years old. The American Egret is much larger than the Snowy Egret and the young Little Blue Heron, but unless the birds are seen together the difference in size may not be apparent at a distance. A difference that can be noted, however, is that the American Egret has a shining yellow bill whereas the Snowy Egret and the immature Little Blue Heron have decidedly dark bills. The American and the Snowy Egret have black legs but the Snowy Egret has yellow feet as an extra feature. This is a point that isn't always visible to the naked eye, however, because the birds are so often seen either on the wing or standing "knee-deep" in water. The Snowy Egret and the immature Little Blue Heron are white birds of approximately the same shape and size but, if you can get close to them, it is not difficult to know which is which. The Snowy Egret is much the daintier bird. Aside from the bright yellow feet of the Snowy Egret that may or may not be visible, the bill and legs are different. Except for a yellow patch at the base, the bill of the Snowy Egret is jet black to the tip. The bill of the Little Blue Heron is a dull lead color and it is thicker than the bill of the smaller Egret. The same comparison may be made of the legs of these two birds. The legs of the Snowy Egret are neat and really black. The legs of the immature Little Blue Heron are a trifle thicker and a rather sickly blue-gray in hue.

The easiest thing to remember is that the largest of these large white wading birds is the American Egret and it has a shining yellow bill as a sure indication of its identity.

[67]

WOOD DUCK
(From 17 to 20 inches)

The male Wood Duck is the most gloriously colored wild bird in North America. Not even the most gaudy of the little Wood Warblers can offer the striking pattern and iridescent hues that the male Wood Duck displays on the lakes, rivers, and woodland ponds of the United States and Canada where it makes its home. The female is a rather plain bird of darkish color with a white patch around the eye that gives it a frightened look at all times. The Wood Duck is quite different from most of our waterfowl. It likes the woods and will perch in trees like a Pigeon. It does not quack. It has a purring whistle for intimate conversation and a buzzing whine for an alarm note. There are a few other members of the Duck family that will nest in holes in trees but the Wood Duck makes a decided habit of it and often the holes are 30 to 40 feet above ground (or water). There are different accounts of how the newly-hatched youngsters get down from the nests to the ground or water below. Some say they flutter down safely and others say that the female carries them down one way or the other, but all agree that the little ones reach water safely within a day or two of hatching. They feed mostly on vegetable matter, with some occasional aquatic insect for dessert. The Wood Duck ranges all over the United States and Canada, going south in Winter only far enough to be sure of open water for feeding purposes. It is a trusting bird, very easily tamed and will return year after year to areas in which it is protected.

CANADA GOOSE
(From 34 to 43 inches)

This is the most abundant Goose of North America, the "honker" of the hunters, the bird that gathers with many others of its kind to migrate in V-formation with Autumn gunners banging away at it when it comes down to earth or water to feed or rest. Though the Canada Goose varies greatly in size, it can hardly be mistaken for any of its wild companions on the water except possibly the Brant, which, though it has the gray-brown body and the black neck and head of the Canada Goose, lacks the clear white "chin-strap" that marks the bigger and better known Canada Goose and its subspecies. These birds have powerful voices and often the great flocks of migrating Canada Geese are heard before they are seen far off in the sky. They spend all their lives in Canada and the United States, breeding in the northerly region and migrating to the more southerly sections when snow and ice cover their Summer homes.

[68]

AMERICAN MERGANSER
(From 21 to 27 inches)

Mergansers are fish-eating members of the Duck family and have narrow saw-toothed bills with which they catch and hold their pray. There are three species of Merganser that are more or less common along our coasts and on the rivers, lakes, and ponds of North America. They are the American, the Red-breasted and the Hooded Merganser, the males of which are all strikingly handsome birds in their "nuptial" or breeding plumage. The females are much duller and much alike in color; grayish birds with reddish-brown heads and gray-white throats and breast. The Hooded Mergansers are much the smaller of the group and the female Hooded may be known by size alone from the similar but noticeably larger females of the American and Red-breasted species. Not only are these two larger females so much alike that only experts can be sure of the difference in the field, but the brilliant males take on that same plumage when the breeding season is over. So there can be plenty of confusion among the Mergansers until the males don their best suits again. But in full plumage, the American Merganser is easily known. It has a shining head of very dark iridescent green, a black back and an all-white body along the water line. The Red-breasted male in the same season is quite different. It is a much darker bird, showing only a white throat and a horizontal white patch in its wing, and wearing the brownish-red broad breast band that gives it the name it carries.

The American and the Hooded Mergansers are more widespread inland than the Red-breasted species, which seems to prefer the regions near the coast. All three Mergansers breed in fresh-water areas but the Red-breasted Mergansers seem to hurry back to salt water as soon as there is a touch of Autumn in the air. They definitely are the most abundant of the migrants and Winter residents in our coastal waters. The American and Hooded Mergansers are just so-so about salt water. They can take it or leave it alone. The Hooded Merganser in particular can leave it alone and, incidentally, the male Hooded Merganser does not go into a dull eclipse of plumage like its larger relatives. It keeps its striking pattern and its ability to raise and lower its handsome crest throughout the year, but it does turn a trifle browner in Autumn, though not enough to confuse anyone who sees it. The male Hooded Merganser is easy to recognize at any time of year.

FLORIDA GALLINULE

(From 12 to 15 inches)

Look in the marshes or around the reedy shores of lakes and ponds for the Florida Gallinule. The "Florida" part of the name is misleading. These birds may be found on or around water almost anywhere in the United States or southern Canada in Summer and anywhere below the ice and snow belt in the United States in Winter. They look strangely like misplaced barnyard fowl as they wander through the reeds or stalk across lily pads, picking at food as they go. Aside from the general dark plumage there is a white line along the lower edge of the wing and a white patch under the tail, but the mark that is as good as a name tag on this bird is the bright red bill with the extension running up the forehead. Unless they are harassed by boys throwing stones or older persons taking shots at them, they often become quite fearless in their Summer homes and go clucking through the reeds with their young like a hen leading a brood of chicks around a dooryard. Despite the fact that their feet are not webbed, they swim readily with a peculiar bobbing of the head.

COOT

(From 13 to 16 inches)

Practically everything that can be said about the Florida Gallinule is also true of the Coot—with one exception! The two birds are about of a size. They have approximately the same shape and general dark color. They live in the same places and have much the same actions and feeding habits. They even swim alike, with a similar bobbing of the head to balance each stroke of the foot. But there is one striking difference that makes it easy

to know the Coot from the Florida Gallinule at any reasonable distance. As the mark of the Florida Gallinule is the bright red bill, the mark of the Coot is the "white nose," the shining white bill with the extension running up the forehead as the red runs up the forehead of the Florida Gallinule. There are other and less noticeable differences between the birds. The Coot is a trifle larger on the average, a little darker on the head, and lacks the white line that the Florida Gallinule displays along the lower edge of the folded wing.

[70]

OSPREY

(From 21 to 24 inches)

Osprey is the official name of this bird but more often it is called a "Fish Hawk," which is a good descriptive name for it because it lives almost exclusively on fish that it catches by plunging feet foremost into the water from a considerable height. It has talons like steel hooks to grasp and hold its prey and often its plunge is so swift that the Osprey disappears completely under the water. When it comes up with a fish—frequently a surprisingly large one—the Osprey shakes the water from its feathers, rests a moment on the surface and then flaps off toward its nest or toward a perch, always holding the fish so that its head is pointing directly in the line of flight.

This is really a magnificent bird. It has a wing-spread of 5 feet or more and is often mistaken for an Eagle because of its size and the fact that its head it largely white. However, the Osprey is clear white underneath, whereas both the Golden Eagle and the Bald Eagle are dark underneath. In fact, the Osprey is the only large bird of prey of North America that is clear white underneath. There really is no mistaking this bird, especially when it is seen in action along our coasts. It may be found over rivers and lakes anywhere in North America but it is much more numerous in the coastal regions where its huge nests atop dead trees, telegraph poles or platforms set out for it are objects that stand out against the skyline. They come back to the same nest year after year and are stubborn about retaining possession. If a nest is destroyed they will rebuild it time and again with sticks, seaweed, cornstalks, and whatever other odd material they can pick up.

There are usually 3 eggs in a clutch and the Ospreys are fond parents to the fledglings. Usually one of the parents stays on or near the nest to protect the young birds while the other is off fishing. Often these birds nest in small colonies and, in the breeding season, the air is full of the clamor of the young and the squealing whistles of the parents. Ospreys are migratory to the extent that they move southward along the coast in Winter, largely because the fish on which they prey head southward as the water becomes colder in the North. Of course, the Ospreys on inland waters have to go south when their northerly feeding range is frozen over. But wherever they may be found, Ospreys are wonderful to watch as they flap along some 50 to 100 feet over the water and then suddenly, sighting a fish below, plummet downard to hit the surface with a great splash, disappear for a few seconds and then come up and fly off with a dinner order of fish.

RED-TAILED HAWK
(From 19 to 25 inches)

Let's face it. There is no doubt that it is often difficult and sometimes impossible for an ordinary observer to know which particular member of the Hawk family is in view. Hawks come in many shapes and sizes and some of them look much alike. There are, however, a few points that may be helpful if kept in mind and there are a few members of the family that are easy to recognize. One of the easy ones is the Red-tailed Hawk, because it has the feature from which it derives its name. The upper surface of its tail is brick red. That might seem a foolish point to mention when the bird is usually seen high overhead, but the Red-tail belongs among the Buteo group of soaring Hawks with broad wings and short, rounded tails. As it soars in wide circles, scanning the ground underneath for sight or sign of prey, its tail is frequently tipped so that the upper surface is visible. It's remarkable how far off and how high overhead this identification mark of the Red-tailed Hawk can be seen, especially when the tail is turned at just the right angle on a sunny day.

Like others of the Buteo group, the Red-tailed Hawk is a much maligned bird. It is usually referred to as a "Chicken Hawk" or a "Hen Hawk" and farmers trap it or shoot it relentlessly. How often have you seen the sides of country barns covered with the carcasses of Hawks? Many of these birds are of the Buteo group and are testimony that the farmer has shot some very good friends, because these Hawks feed mostly on mice and other small mammals that are harmful on farm lands. The smaller Hawks of the Accipitrine group, which are bird catchers by profession, are the ones that do the most damage around the poultry yard. They dash in quickly and disappear with a chick or a broiler. The farmer hears or sees the excitement but the criminal has disappeared with the booty. Overhead is a Red-tail sailing around calmly, looking for mice. The farmer shakes his fist at the Red-tail, vows vengeance and takes it with a shotgun at the first chance. If the farmer knew one Hawk from another, he wouldn't slaughter his friends in that fashion. He would wait to catch the real criminal, which might be a Goshawk, a Cooper's Hawk or a Sharp-shinned Hawk.

The Red-tailed Hawk is a permanent resident over almost all of North America but some of the birds of the more northerly wilds move a bit southward in Winter to find better weather and a readier supply of food. As is the case with most birds of prey, the female is quite a bit larger than the male. The call is a loud husky squeal, something like escaping steam from a small valve. A bird much like the Red-tailed Hawk is its near relative, the Red-shouldered Hawk, which is almost as large as the Red-tail but lacks that "signboard" of the red tail, has a ruddy tinge on its under-parts and has a clear ringing "kee-you" cry as it soars in circles overhead.

COOPER'S HAWK
(From 14 to 20 inches)

Among the North American Hawks there are three close relatives that are winged terrors. They are the Goshawk, the Cooper's Hawk and the Sharp-shinned Hawk, members of the Accipitrine group, and they dine on wild birds or barnyard fowl with equal relish. They also eat mice, squirrels, and rabbits on occasion, but most of their food is feathered and includes song birds, game birds and farm poultry. The Accipitrine Hawks have short, rounded wings and long tails and they fly by alternately flapping rapidly and sailing. The Goshawk, much the largest of the three, is a grayish bird, northerly in distribution, never common, and seen mostly in Winter in the United States. The Cooper s Hawk and the Sharp-shinned Hawk, common throughout the United States and Canada, are blue-gray above and whitish below with red-brown cross barring. They are almost identical in everything except size and the shape of the ends of their tails. The Cooper's Hawk is the larger and has a rounded tail. The "Sharpy" has a square tail.

SPARROW HAWK
(From 9 to 12 inches)

This lovely little representative of the famous Falcon family is not, on the average, much larger than a Robin but it is a typical Falcon in flight, wheeling and turning sharply and darting swiftly through the air, often uttering the high-pitched "killy-killy-killy" cry that gives it the name of "Killy Hawk" in some localities. It lives largely on insects, worms and mice but it may occasionally catch a few small birds in Winter when other food is difficult to find. The general body color of the Sparrow Hawk is a rich pinkish-brown above and lighter below, with a plentiful sprinkling of dark cross-bars, streaks and spots. The smaller male is easily known by its blue-gray wings. From other small Hawks the Sparrow Hawks are distinguished by the two black vertical stripes on the whitish sides of their heads. A larger relative of this delightful and handsome little Hawk is the Peregrine Falcon or Duck Hawk, a noble bird and the fastest feathered flier in North America.

BOB-WHITE
(About 10 inches)

The Bob-white, which keeps calling its name clearly over and over again so that there will be no mistake about it, is a Quail and the best known of that family over the central and eastern sections of North America. Quail are small round birds like plump, short-legged Chickens and they have much the same feeding habits as Chickens. In general the Bob-white is reddish-brown with many dark bars and spots. The male has a clear white throat and a clear white line over the eye. In the female the throat and line over the eye are buffy. Except in the breeding season, Bob-whites go about in small groups called bevies and in the bevy they have a remarkable sleeping arrangement. They sit in a tight circle on the ground, all tails together in the center and their heads making the outer rim of the circle. They are placed like spokes in a wheel. If they are attacked in the darkness by a fox, raccoon, skunk, or prowling house cat, they immediately fly off the way they are headed, which means in all directions. That's the reason for this odd way of gathering for sleep. It's a safety device.

CALIFORNIA QUAIL
(About 10 inches)

There is no difficulty in identifying the friendly little California Quail with its quaint nodding plume dangling over its forehead as it feeds in the fields, orchards, and kitchen gardens of the Far West. The only bird with which it might be confused is the Gambel's Quail, quite similar in color and general pattern and wearing practically the same picturesque plume. But the Gambel's Quail has a bright chestnut-reddish crown and, in the middle of its lighter lower breast, it has a distinct black patch like a large inkspot. Not only are these differences easily noted but the Gambel's Quail is largely a bird of the desert regions of the Southwest, whereas the California Quail is much more widespread over the Rocky Mountain and Pacific Coast region and is so familiar a bird around inhabited areas that it is often seen in public parks and even vacant lots in California towns.

[74]

RUFFED GROUSE
(From 16 to 19 inches)

If you go walking in the woods and a big brownish bird starts up almost underfoot with an explosive whirr of wings that scares the wits out of you, that will be the Ruffed Grouse, the finest upland game bird of North America. It has a decided preference for the woods or brush-covered country and rarely ventures into the open where there is no thick cover in which it can quickly disappear. If you happen to see it walking on the floor of the forest it will look like a short-legged, plump, dark brown barnyard hen with mottled plumage. There are many kinds of Grouse in different parts of the world and we have seven or eight species in the United States and Canada. Of these the best known and most widely distributed is the Ruffed Grouse that gets its name from the "ruff" of greenish-black feathers sprouting from the base of the neck and draped over the shoulders of the bird. The male wears the larger and shinier ruff and it can be fluffed out in courtship or when challenging some rival male. It's the male, too, that does the famous drumming, an odd sound often heard where these birds are plentiful. It is done partly to allure the female and partly to challenge male rivals. The performances are more numerous in the Spring, but it has been heard at all times of the year and at all hours of the day and night. The male Ruffed Grouse picks out a stump or log for a regular drumming platform and then begins the performance, which is all done with its wings. The drumming starts like a series of slow, heavy thumps and gradually increases in rapidity until it is a hollow roll at the finish. Sometimes a bird will drum every five minutes or so for an hour at a time and often the drumming of one male will be answered by the drumming of another at a distance.

The female lays from 7 to 15 eggs in a depression on the ground in the woods and the young follow the mother off the nest as soon as they are hatched. It isn't long before the little ones sprout enough flight feathers to be able to flutter to low branches for safety if the brood is attacked by a fox, a lynx or a hunting house-cat. If you come upon a mother with young, the mother will often attempt to frighten you off by rushing at you with all her feathers raised. If that fails, she will flop away as if her wing were broken, trying to lure you away from the place in which the young are crouched motionless and invisible on the ground.

The Ruffed Grouse is a hardy bird that is able to get along in rugged country through the coldest weather and the deepest snows of Winter. A curious feature is that in the snowy season its toes sprout little hair-like fringes that help it to walk over soft snow. The delicate tracks of these fringes may be seen in the snow under haw bushes and other such spots where the Ruffed Grouse gather to feed in the Winter.

[75]

TURKEY VULTURE

(From 26 to 32 inches)

The Turkey Vulture must be the champion non-stop glider of the feathered world. It soars the skies ceaselessly, a huge blackish bird that looks as big as an Eagle and often circles over the same area for an hour without once flapping its wings. The Golden Eagle and the immature Bald Eagle—before it has developed the white head and tail—also look like huge blackish birds at any distance in flight but there is no need to mistake a Turkey Vulture for an Eagle on that account. The Eagles are uniformly dark on the under side of their wings but there is a two-tone pattern to the wings of the Turkey Vulture that is an easy mark of identification when the bird is circling overhead. The forward half of the wing is the same blackish color as the rest of the bird's plumage but the rear half is a tan-brown that stands out by contrast. The dividing line is sharp and the distinct two-tone pattern usually is quite clear when the bird makes a favorable turn in the air. Since the Turkey Vulture circles much of the time, it usually isn't long before it makes a turn that provides a good glimpse of the under side of the wings.

Because of the bare red skin of its upper neck and head and its custom of feeding on dead animals, garbage, and other such tidbits, the Turkey Vulture sometimes is looked upon as a repulsive bird. It is not a thing of beauty nor is it a singer to be compared with the Mockingbird. About all it utters is an occasional croak or sharp hiss when disturbed. But it is valuable as a scavenger. It is an unpaid but very willing worker in any clean-up campaign around the country. In fact, it is in such good repute as a feathered "street cleaner" that it is protected by law in many sections. If there is a dead horse in a field or a dead fox in the woods, the Vultures will find it quickly and gather to dispose of the remains in their own way. Sometimes they feast so strenuously that they take on too much weight and can't lift themselves from the ground when they try to take off in flight. In that case they readily disgorge some of the banquet, a habit that gives them another black mark for horrible table manners. They often gather around the city dumps by the dozens in the southern part of the United States, the region in which they are most abundant. They may be found as residents over much of the country, though they prefer the southern half. They are hardy individuals, however, that push as far north as the Canadian border region all the way from Maine to the Pacific Coast.

The first cousin of the Turkey Vulture is the somewhat smaller Black Vulture that doesn't range as widely as its larger relative. It keeps mostly to the southeastern and south central part of the United States. The bare skin of its upper neck and head is not red but a grubby pearl-gray or even darker color. Its tail is noticeably shorter than that of the Turkey Vulture, which is much the more graceful bird in the air.

BALD EAGLE

(From 30 to 34 inches)

Everybody knows the Bald Eagle, the national bird of the United States that is famous in song and story, but not everybody realizes that many Bald Eagles in the air show no signs of "baldness" and are often mistaken for Golden Eagles, which never grow "bald" or white-headed. The mistake occurs because it takes young Bald Eagles from three to four years to acquire the white head and tail by which the species is so well known and easily recognized. Through their junior years Bald Eagles wear a complete costume of mottled dark brown that makes them look black at a distance and, since young Golden Eagles are much the same color and only slightly larger in size, except for experts in the field there is much confusion in identifying immature Eagles. But when the Bald Eagle comes of age and dons the white head and white tail of its tribe, all confusion ends.

Benjamin Franklin bitterly opposed the selection of the Bald Eagle as the emblem of the United States. He insisted it was a disreputable bird that made a living as a robber, taking from other and weaker birds the food they had garnered for themselves. Franklin favored the Wild Turkey as our national bird. He contended that the Turkey had none of the vices of the Bald Eagle, was a self-supporting bird and, in addition, was good to eat. Others have spoken worse of the Bald Eagle than Benjamin Franklin did. It is accused of having carried off and devoured little children, but such stories are regarded as fairy tales.

It's true that Bald Eagles will engage in armed robbery, threatening lesser birds with their terrific talons and making them yield up the food they are carrying. Ospreys are frequent victims of such air raids because they catch fish and Eagles dote on fish. The Bald Eagle haunts lakes, rivers, and ocean shores, feeding eagerly on fish of any kind, large or small, dead or alive, honestly earned or boldly stolen. It will also roam the hills and eat small mammals, frogs, snakes, lizards and anything else that it can catch. It has some faults but it is a majestic bird of great dignity, noble bearing and wonderful powers of flight. Of such a bird it was well written by Alfred Tennyson:

> *He clasps the crag with crooked hands;*
> *Close to the sun in lonely lands,*
> *Ring'd with the azure world, he stands.*
> *The wrinkled sea beneath him crawls;*
> *He watches from his mountain walls,*
> *And like a thunderbolt he falls.*

Such is the way of Eagles.